Weighing Up

Weighing Up

George Scales, 1985

To Michael
With every good wish
George Scales
Hyde Park 1989

WEIGHING UP

George Scales

*Illustrated by
Colin White*

Journeyman/T&GWU

First published by the Journeyman Press, 1988
in collaboration with the Transport & General Workers Union

The Journeyman Press Limited, 97 Ferme Park Road
Crouch End, London, N8 9SA and
Journeyman/Kampmann & Company Inc, 9 East 40th Street
New York, NY 10016

Transport & General Workers Union, Transport House
Smith Square, London, SW1P 3JB

The photographs by Douglas Lawson have been
reproduced with the kind permission of his Estate and
the Ashgrove Press, publisher of *Hand to the Plough: Old
Farm Tools and Machinery in Pictures* by Douglas
Lawson, 1982

ISBN 1 85172 023 5

First printing 1988

10 9 8 7 6 5 4 3 2 1

Cover illustration by Ingrid van der Gucht

Typeset by Wordstream Ltd, Poole
printed by Richard Clay Ltd, Bungay, Suffolk

Foreword

'I'VE BEEN a builder, electrician, carpenter, mechanic, vet and stockman,' said Howard the farmworker. 'Never wanted to settle in a job?' I asked, marvelling at his versatility. 'Settle be blowed,' came the answer, 'that's just the work I did yesterday!'

The chocolate box picture of popular imagination — the simple farm labourer and the rural idyll — has always been a fiction. Farmworker George Scales has one extra talent for which we should all give thanks. An extraordinary ability to write, which unambiguously sweeps away the myth, and instead evokes the real flavour of agricultural work and life in a rural community.

Every month for six years from 1979, regular as clockwork, there dropped a white envelope on to the doormat at Headland House — the headquarters of the National Union of Agricultural and Allied Workers. It contained George's column for the *Landworker*, meticulously typed to the allotted length.

A joy to read, it would require no subediting.

Working as I was on the *Landworker*, it was a monthly treat to be savoured for its imagination and professionalism. Over the years the column acquired such a following and renown that an emergency resolution was passed at a farmworkers' union conference forbidding George from retiring from his column. Thus was born 'Carrying On', the successor to 'Weighing Up'. All praise, then, to Francis Beckett, editor of the *Landworker* when George was given his niche in the union paper, for having the guts to inaugurate a column by a lay member of the NUAAW.

But the Scales' talents are unique. A sharp eye and ear, an unwavering sense of injustice, and a pencil kept in his gumboot for jotting down thoughts — all these informed his monthly parables. They combined the timeless feel of a cracking good yarn with the immediacy of contemporary concerns. They mixed a superb narrative with an acid wit — oiling the message with humour.

His subjects ranged from the perils of working with unpredictable animals, incredible colleagues and miserable bosses, to the grinding poverty of rural workers and his belief in the union's role in standing up for the rights and dignity of working men and women.

George, who has selected the material printed in this book, is equally at home upsetting farmers and farmworkers. He attacks farmers who have grown rich on the backs of their workers whilst paying them poverty level wages. 'It's the injustice of it. The blokes who put in all the work get nothing. Finish up nowhere. The farmers get the lot. When the boss takes a holiday nobody misses him. If a worker is off there's complete panic.'

But farmworkers who praise village schools, tied cottages and ploughing contests get the rough side of George's tongue as well.

'All psalms and sea shanties' was the eary Scales' recollection of the village school he attended in Hertfordshire. The year 1931, at the age of eleven, saw him joining a school in Welwyn Garden City which had a socialist schoolmaster.

It was a good break, and it gave George the taste for reading which he kept with him during his four years in a steelworks, and subsequently in the army. He remembers sixpenny books from the Rationalist Press by Samuel Butler, H G Wells, Bertrand Russell, J B S Haldane and Professor Joad (later of 'Brains Trust' fame).

'I went in the army and some silly bugger started a war!' explains George. He spent the start of the Second World War in the desert in Egypt with the Royal Engineers. Claiming not to be any good at anything else George took up cartooning, 'scribbling' and poetry, acquiring something of a reputation for lampooning officers.

On his demob he was about to go into a printing job in Ipswich when he took a breather on a public bench in Welwyn. 'It was the most beautiful March weather. Food was rationed, people were yearning for bread, the Land Army was being dissolved and the PoWs repatriated. I plumped for working on the land.'

Farmworkers have always had the dirty end of the stick. For years they have been told by successive governments and the farmers' own union, the NFU, if you'll only increase your productivity, and adapt to new work practices, your wage packets will grow as fat as the people you are feeding.

Now, a land army pared to the bone, operating complex and dangerous machinery and chemicals — and like the livestock, worth a king's ransom — is still paid so badly for long hours that large numbers have to claim state benefit.

George Scales leaves you in no doubt where he stands.

Now enjoy the read.

Chris Kaufman
Editor, *T&G Record*
June 1988

When praising the Lord for his harvest
    Remember the sinners who gathered it in
For if it were left to the pure and the holy
    We would all be excessively thin.

Starting at the Bottom
and Working Downwards

 THIS IS a new venture; I hope it sticks. If it doesn't I hope the blame is entirely my own. Things do go wrong, though sometimes it's difficult to see why.

Take the *Landworker* book review feature for example: that budded but never bloomed. Was it because books are so expensive nowadays and priced beyond the reach of farmworkers' pockets? Or did the editor overrate his readers' keenness for books? Whatever it was, he should be commended for trying to raise some interest in them.

Personally, I like books, because they allow the humble to sit down with the mighty. What's more, if he feels that way inclined, the humble reader can, by skipping a page or two, hurry the sage along if he thinks the great one is talking rubbish. I've gone even further. At one time or another, I've slung Churchill, Montgomery, Kipling and Tennyson out the back door for talking out the top of their noble heads . . . and not one of them complained!

I think at this stage in my column, it would be helpful to the reader if I mentioned something about my roots. A mini potted-history, so to speak.

I was born, three weeks overdue, on Good Friday, a day after All Fools' Day in 1920. Unplanned for, I arrived in the middle of one of the wettest nights on record. Dad had to bike four miles through the rain to fetch the midwife. He was well-nigh drowned, and never forgave me for not holding on a while till it eased up a little. Mum was none too pleased with me either. She wanted a girl but got another boy who, unlike her first was, in her own words, a grizzle-guts and as ugly as sin.

Tied cottage

That was my start in life. However, as bad as it was, it could have been worse. Just imagine being born prematurely — a girl, with my looks, and an April fool at that!

I lived in a tied cottage right from the start and got most of my education at a Church of England school. Which was the greater drawback of the two I wouldn't care to say. I'd abolish both! 'Rent books not Hymn books!' has forever been my battle-cry.

My schooling was not intended to be extended. Dad's pay packet saw to that. Even so, neither mum nor dad rated education very highly; so mine ceased as soon as they could legally end it.

At the bottom

When I left school, mistakenly thinking that if you

start at the very bottom you can't help but go upwards, I got myself a job as a rivetter's mate's labourer, but couldn't hold it down, and finished up on the dole. That was why I joined the Army. Soldiers don't get sacked — they only get shot! Without my asking, the Army gave me the rank of sapper (that's another word for private, or general labourer), a ring-side seat for World War Two, and when I got demobbed, a trilby hat which I never wore.

George *(leaning on the mudguard)* at HM Government's Rehabilitation Scheme for Ex-Servicemen, near Peterborough, winter 1946–47

Back in Civvy Street without a job, I fell easy prey to a local farmer on the prowl for cheap labour. He took me on under the war-time Government's rehabilitation of ex-servicemen scheme. Then went very close to rupturing me — but taught me nothing.

Sorry! I malign the man. He taught me two

things . . . how well farmers stick together and how they hate their workers doing the same.

If he hadn't put me right on that, I would never be writing this. Nor anything else, for that matter, which extols the virtues of unity among workers. But more about that some other time.

Buried Alive

HAVING LAID a wreath on its grave, it's spookey, to say the least, to see so soon the resurrection of the *Landworker's* 'Books' feature. In future, I'll hold a colder mirror a little closer to the assumed corpse's mouth before ordering a wreath.

That sort of undue hastiness on my part reminds me of a wartime incident in the desert late one night when I was stung by a scorpion.

Thinking it to be lethal, at something more than a leisurely trot, I made for my unit's medical centre (a bell-tent and a small bottle of smelling salts.) But since the orderly there knew as little as I did about scorpion stings, he agreed to accompany me at the double to the nearest regimental aid post. (Two bell-tents and a large bottle of smelling salts.)

On arriving there, we found the duty-officer's light-hearted approach to my case quite upsetting. After giving me an aspirin, he told me to report back in the morning if the sting was still troubling me.

'In the morning?' my companion screeched, in utter dismay. 'He'll be dead by then.'

'Dead? Why dead?' the officer calmly asked.

'Well, last week another mate of ours was stung – and within a couple of hours he was . . . '

'Don't tell me he died?'

'I hope so,' the orderly said, 'we buried him!'

Grace and Flavour

 BEING THE clear minded fellow he is, I'm surprised George Curtis brackets me with George Edwards. Surely he recognises the real difference between a reed and an oak; and realises that someone like me needs something more substantial than hymns — be they Ancient and Modern or Sankey and Moody — to fortify him and carry him through the trials and tribulations of life?

In fairness to George and other readers with strong religious beliefs, I may as well reveal, right here and now, that I lost my passion for the Christian way of life way back in distant childhood.

Lost it, quite irretrievably, on the very day my mother clouted my ears for declaring, as we sat down to a frugal meal, that we could do with less grace and more gravy.

From that moment on, for me, the command, 'Suffer! Little children' has had an insidious ring about it.

Unpopular Front

‘That’s the closest I’ve come to a Victory,’ he said
At the Poll, as he counted the cost
And tore up his spurned Manifesto
And mourned the deposit he’d lost.

Lean-ometer Wanted

ANY ARTICLE about working trac-tors across slopes (such as the one in April's *Landworker*) has me sitting up and taking notice; because, with pounding heart, I've been forced to trundle tractors with trepidation across some steep enough to hang pictures on — and it hasn't been fun.

There is, however, a solution to the problem of how to avoid tractors toppling over on steep slopes. It's simplicity in itself; and it should have been adopted years ago.

Cabs are fitted with gauges telling drivers when they are running out of fuel: so, why not a lean-ometer telling them when they are running out of luck?

Nothing elaborate is needed. Just a simple, easy-to-see device, motivated by gravity, which would not only show the driver how far his tractor is leaning from upright but would also prove to the boss that his tractor driver is being sensible for refusing to work across a gradient that would bring a mountain goat out in a cold sweat.

Gravy Galore!

 WHERE GRAVY is concerned, I'm sure Brother Holliday (Letters, June *Landworker*) will be interested to know that I'm very much like the old farmworker who, when he was sheltering from a storm and discussing the question of reincarnation with a mate, said although he could see some merit in coming back as a dolphin — as it wasn't bothered by wet weather — he'd prefer not to, as he didn't fancy drowning his grub in gravy.

The Wrong Pay Packet

ACCORDING TO the tables given with Reg Groves' story about the Wages Board, it seems that in the 20s my father's old boss was paying dad two bob a week over the odds. This rather surprises me as his boss had quite a reputation for being an old skin-flint. Without speculating as to why he got the extra, all it meant was — that after stoppages for rent and what he called 'Lloyd George's', dad used to bring home the grand sum of 28/6 (£1.42) for the seven of us to live on: a little over 4/- (20p) per head per week.

Another disgraceful but interesting thing the tables reveal is the lack of concern on the part of the farmers for the welfare of their workers throughout the decade they cover.

Fortunately for us, unlike those whose breadwinner had to stay on the land, our family didn't have to wait until 1938 for that paltry 4/- a week extra. By pure chance we were living in the very area Ebenezer Howard chose for his second Garden City and farmland was being taken over for development. When dad's place of work came under the hammer he seized the opportunity it gave him to show agriculture a clean pair of heels; and he was off like a shot to a better paid job in one of the new factories.

That was in 1928; and, as a better paid man in a better paying county, he had been well-off compared with most farmworkers. Even so, the change when it came was almost beyond belief.

I remember dad returning home fairly late every night that first week, and on the Friday (pay-day) after hanging up his dinner bag, his cap and his coat, all smiles, he handed mum a remarkably bulky pay packet. She took it — and felt its fullness. Now, as she had never felt the thickness of two Treasury notes tucked one in the other in a pay packet before, she instantly became suspicious and handed it back to dad.

'They've given you the wrong one, mate,' she said. 'They've given you someone else's by mistake. Either it's that, or they're testing your honesty ... I bet that's what they're up to. Take it back, and ask them for yours!'

Dad's smile left his face as quickly as he had left the land.

'What d'ya mean ... the wrong one? It's mine all right. It's got my clocking-in number on it ... ain't it?'

'Maybe it has. But it all seems fishy to me. There's over four pounds in it. That's more than twice the amount you've been getting. Take it back. I shan't rest till you do.'

To settle the matter dad took it back the next day, but made a special trip home during his dinner-break to bring news to mum. Taking the packet from his pocket he said: 'It *is* mine! Now go out and spend it! And for Christ's sake let's have some butter on our bread for a change!'

I shall never forget the way mum reacted to dad's wonderful news. As she counted and fondled the four, crisp pound notes and several silver coins, she exclaimed: 'Whatever have you been doing to deserve all this!'

Then she burst into tears. And that, apart from the time when she spilled a basin of boiling hot fat over her hand, was the only time in my life I can ever remember seeing my mother cry.

Bright Boy's Capers

FARMING IS a dirty, dusty, dangerous and very often deafening occupation. It's nothing like the glamorous romp-in-the-hay affair that television and radio people make it out to be. That is why, even after allowing for the fact that programme compilers have a living to make and must always be on the lookout for the unusual, I'll offer no marks at all to the BBC's 'Nationwide' team for publicising, almost drooling over, the accomplishments of a farmer's schoolboy son who was shown driving a combine harvester — an awesome machine of great complexity — while his father was having a break.

The commentator ended the piece by saying: 'As would be expected, the lad intends to become a farmer when he grows up.' I suppose he will. Provided, of course, his luck holds out!

Personally, I'm more concerned about the effect the little starlet had on other young children, rather than his own future, because he couldn't have come on at a worse time: slap bang in the middle of harvest and the school holidays; the very time one would expect the BBC to be warning against, not applauding, a young child climbing onto and setting into motion a dangerous farm machine.

Change and Changeless

UNLIKE OUR ex-president, Brother Bert Hazell, who once told an Essex Conference which had accused him of siding with the farmers that he never read the thing, I have been reading the *Farmers Weekly* since it was first published.

I have never taken to the way it looks over the top of its spectacles at anything we farmworkers do that is not dead in line with the farmers' bidding. Nevertheless, in fairness, I must say I find many of its articles interesting and educational. There was one recently which I found particularly so.

The article was to do with a collection of cards, stamps and postmarks, dating back to 1785. Four of the cards were reprinted: and as we are near to the time of the Wages Board settlement, I thought two of them were appropriate to the occasion.

One showed a harvest field in 1910, swarming with workers bringing home the sheaves. The other made quite clear that the end result of all that human effort, in terms of productivity, is puny when it's set beside today's expectations.

It would seem that since those days, while the workforce has been halved, halved, and halved again, yields have gone up and up and up. Needless to say, there the comparison ends. For in those days farmworkers were the lowest paid in the land.

We still are!

Some things never change.

Grace and Old Lace

 I GET fed up with workers from other industries telling me where our weakness lies and why we always get less than the little we ask for. Put in a similar position, I doubt whether they'd do any better. It's one thing fighting a boss you have never met, at long range; quite another to get scrapping with one who lives next door and owns the house you live in. Yet, for all that, down the ages, there has always been 'Some village Hampden that with dauntless breast the little tyrant of his fields withstood . . .'

And the 'Hampden' I have in mind whenever I read those lines from Gray's famous elegy takes the form of a woman I knew — Grace Munday.

Grace was married to a farmworker; a genial fellow, who put all his trust in merit, hoping that in time, it would be richly rewarded. Grace had other ideas, and she wasn't afraid of letting them be known at places and times where they mattered most — mainly, but not always in the fields when piece-work rates for casual workers were being fixed.

There was the time in the 1920s when her outspokenness shattered the calm of a WI meeting in our village hall. To make matters worse, it was a special meeting; for it was graced by the awesome presence of none other than Lady X, the wife of an aristocratic land owner; who, naturally enough, had been given the honour of handing the prizes for that month's competition − for the best prepared table cloth − which, quite unexpectedly, Grace won by a handsome margin.

This was not a popular win. For one thing, Grace was a new member and for another she had, in the past, said some harsh things about Mrs. Nancy Puke, the wife of the farmer for whom Grace's husband worked.

When the congratulatory platitudes had been said, Grace was called onto the platform to receive her prize: a detachable, lace collar − all the fashion in those days. She took it, and was returning to her place when a strange curiosity seemed to overcome her. At the platform edge she stopped, took a more discerning look at the collar, wheeled around and stepped straight back to the top table again.

Dangling her prize at arm's length right under Mrs. Puke's nose, she exclaimed: 'This is one of old Nancy's left-offs. I've seen her wearing it! This is no first prize . . . it's jumble sale stuff . . . I wouldn't use it as a duster. You can have it back. I'll take my table cloth, and be on my way.' And with that, she left.

An uneasy silence gripped the hall. Then, regaining their composure, the VIPs conferred and decided that Grace must be brought back and made to apologise. An envoy was sent and arrived to find Grace already waiting at her door.

'I have been expecting you,' said Grace, 'What do you want?'

'You — to come and apologise. You ought to; it's a beautiful collar and must have cost a lot when it was new ...'

Forty years later, I asked Grace if she remembered the incident.

'Yes,' she said, 'the rumpus it caused too. Some said I made a fool of myself, but I don't think I did. You would have done the same ... surely you would?

I'm not so sure. I wonder ... ?

---

* The names are as fictitious as the people were real!

Unlucky for Some

Arriving in Heaven a little bit late.
  He said to St. Peter as he passed through the gate:
'The funeral benefit I got was so small,
  I could hardly afford the fare here at all.
And if inflation continues, it grieves me to tell,
  My mates won't be coming — they'll be going to *Hell*!'

Breathe Free

 THE BANNER headline to April's *Landworker* should leave no doubt in anyone's mind — least of all Peter Walker's — where the Union stands regarding weed-killer 245T. It's heartening as well as inspiring to see the Union taking a lead in this matter. That, to me, is the kind of thing the Union should be doing; seeing a wrong and setting about putting it right, and in the case of the weed-killer, I'm sure it won't be long before the issue is put right. Soon the pressures that are being brought to bear on it will be taking effect. We shall then see the banning of that insidious spray and see those people who come into contact with it and are likely to be affected by it, breathing freely again.

What a pity it is that close (on the next page) to the highly commendable piece of campaigning we find these same far-sighted people who have been putting so much effort into up-dating twentieth century thinking, reverting to forelock-tugging attitudes that should have been buried long ago with Queen Victoria. I'm referring, of course, to the *Landworker* report on the long service awards that are planned to take place at this year's Three Counties Show.

Docility Medals

So, what's wrong with reporting on that forthcoming event, you might ask? Nothing at all — it's just the tone of it that grates. The event itself leaves me cold. I can't think of anything good about long-service-in-farming Medals at all. They are a mockery and in the interests of truth should be called Docility Medals. Where farmers are concerned they are nothing but a patronising indulgence, and on our part the seal of our submissiveness.

Just think for one moment of those people at whose behest we receive those baubles — at the time when we are about to shut the farm gate behind us for the last time and head into the fast setting sun. Are these short term benefactors not the long term malefactors who throughout our working lives have been constantly objecting to and thwarting every social advancement we have tried to make? Who, in protest, churlishly walked out of the Wages Board meeting last November because their workers were being offered slightly over half the amount the Union had asked for?

Are they not the people who dislike rules that add to their workers' comfort and safety? Who kicked the tied cottage law into a shape that now guarantees them cheap labour for ever more? Of course they are. We owe them nothing! We certainly shouldn't apologetically worry about the ever increasing cost of a silver medal or drool over an added bonus of £30 for the recipient from the over-spilling coffers of the corn merchants and the building societies. On such sad occasions the thought of bonuses should not enter our minds.

At County Shows, for the shame of it, I make a point of hurrying past the Grand Ring when such presentations are in the offing. The thought of those old timers obediently waiting there in line, like Bob-tailed English Sheepdogs, not quite knowing whether they're going to get a Bob Martins on the tongue, or a Dr Martens up the rear, fills me with boundless fury and does nothing for my blood pressure, which, in turn makes my chance of ever living long enough to be one day standing on such hallowed ground more remote than even I wish it to be.

On Snobs

A LETTER, signed 'Landlubber' appeared in the farming press at the beginning of August complaining about the city snobs who have moved into the Milton Keynes area. The writer was quite upset about them and cited a few cases.

Now although I can appreciate his annoyance, I can't understand his surprise. Toffee-nosed townies didn't bring snobbery into the countryside. It was invented here. I remember writing some time ago about the hierarchy of the horsemen of old and the little corporals of our industry. We lack nothing where snobbery is concerned.

At gymkhanas, horses play a secondary role to it. Flower shows, garden parties and coffee mornings are tailored to fit it. The trouble with snobbery is that the lower you are in the pecking order, the fewer people you are likely to meet worse off than yourself to practice it on. Nevertheless they can be found if you make a keen enough search.

When they closed our village school in 1929 and we pupils were transferred to a 'posher' one in town, our new schoolmaster, thinking perhaps that we needed something more uplifting in the way of culture than a bit of ferreting on a Sunday after-noon, started violin classes after school hours. Six-pence a session. The instruments to be paid for on the never-never. Not surprisingly there weren't any takers among our lot. Farmworkers' wages in those days didn't run to such cultural luxuries.

Nonetheless, the woman across the way, Mrs Mills the head cowman's wife, who was a snob of the first order, not to be outdone and wanting to impress the day labourers' wives, bought her daughter Cicely a second-hand violin case and told her to take her time coming home from school with it on practice nights.

Sad to say when the girl disobeyed another instruction and opened it in full view of her class-mates, culture took a bit of a dip. There's a world of difference between a Stradivarius and a bottle of cold tea and slice of bread and jam.

But the woman knew no shame. A few weeks later the farm foreman's wife invited Cicely and the second cowman's son Bertie to their son John's birthday party. Bertie called for Cicely before she was ready. So he was invited inside to wait — closely watched by Mrs Mills.

The boy sniffed. The woman pricked her ears. Then raising her eyebrows asked: 'Haven't you been given a handkerchief?' 'No,' he admitted. 'Goodness gracious me!' She exclaimed. 'You just can't go to John's without one.' And turning to her daughter bade her 'Lend him one of yours ... we can burn it afterwards.'

Beef Dripping

I'M NOT going to talk about talented people; only about farm managers. About myself, in fact, and how within forty-eight hours of becoming a manager my pride took a ghastly knock.

I was given notice of my promotion Friday dinner time. By tea time on Saturday I had kitted myself out to look the part; hacking jacket, cavalry twill trousers, soft-collared pastel-shaded shirt (with matching tie), brown market boots — commonly known as beetle-crushers — and, of course, a cap of loudest check. Thus attired, on Sunday morning I went out to meet the boss and a livestock dealer to argue the possible sale of some forward stores.

I'd arrived! A manager at last! So naturally I took up a manager's stance and tried to look as though my next assignment after selling the stores was to ring up the Biblical Society and get the Ten Commandments amended. But you cannot have such lofty aspirations and a Cockney mother-in-law as well . . .

Just as I was beginning to become puffed up with my own importance and bloated with self-esteem, mine paid me an unexpected visit. She arrived by car. As it parked she lowered the window, thrust out her hand clutching a pudding basin and yelled: 'I've brought your dripping George!'

'Did she say dripping, Scales?' the boss asked.

'She did,' I answered, then trying to regain a little of my lost poise, added ' . . . best beef.'

'Sniv' Contest

AT THE moment I'm busy promoting a competition of my own . . . a 'Sniv of the Century' contest.

But before any of you rush to send in your nomination papers and your entry money, I'd better warn you that competition will be of the highest order; and to give you some idea of what I mean by that, let me straight away introduce you to my own nominee who, I think, will be among the front runners right from the word go.

Will Croucher (that's the name of my super-sniv) lived in a cottage situated by a gravel track which led from the farm house to the farm itself. In fact the cottage stood just where the track met the concrete apron around the farm buildings, and because of the constant pounding there from the traffic which bumped off the concrete and on to the track, a depression had formed that collected water from the apron and elsewhere. In fact we had a puddle. A sizeable one that went right across the track, was a stride and a half in width and quite deep too.

Now Will used to keep a Passchendale-type duckboard handy, and at weekends — that was the time when the big boss and his family visited the farm — Will would watch unseen for their approach and as they neared the puddle, would hurry out with the duckboard and lay it over the water, thus allowing them to cross, dry-footed, to the other side.

'He is one of the old school. The salt of the earth.'

That in itself was bad enough, but to me the really sickening part of it was the way Will used to slop about in the puddle steadying the board with one hand and the people on top with the other . . . all the while saying how nice it was to see them about the place and how he hoped they would find everything to their liking, bowing so low as he spoke, he rippled the murky water with his chin.

'Croucher's so thoughtful,' the missus would say to the boss, as they disappeared into one of the buildings. 'Yes,' he'd reply, 'He is one of the old school. The salt of the earth.'

What they didn't know, however, was that this particular block of salt kept a dipstick as well as a duckboard, and in drying weather he used to nip out and test the depth of the puddle. If it showed any signs of drying out, early on Saturday morning when nobody was about, he'd set to and top it up.

Fewer Workers

QUITE A fair proportion of my overtime money has gone on books trying to discover why some do so little for so much, while others do so much for so little — yet the mystery remains. However, there came a fleeting moment in my life when I thought I'd made the break-through, whereby I could double my income without having to bolt my food or snatch my sleep in the process. That was in 1954.

'You come and work regularly for me, George,' said a farmer one day when I was doing a little job for him on the side. 'Forget about the hours, there's £500 a year for you and if the farm does well I'll double it. It'd be silly not to!' Such an offer I couldn't resist: so within a fortnight I became his head tractor man.

I sadly realised by breakfast time on the first morning when I saw the job sheet that I'd made a misjudgement of the same magnitude as Jack Boddy's when, just after taking office, he said: 'The NUAAW is an independent union and has been for

A break from drilling grass seed, Waltham Cross, 1954

71 years. I anticipate we will remain an independent union for the next 71 years.'

Anyway, that's beside the point. The lesson I want to pass on, particularly to the younger reader, is to steer clear of open-ended agreements: a defined wage for undefined hours.

Mark you, I wasn't the only worker there in 1954 enduring that bitter lesson. Over the year there were quite a number. Especially cowmen. What with three times a day milking and being called upon between-whiles to unload lorries, to help with the pigs and poultry, they never did seem able to raise their eye-lids high enough for me to catch the colour of their eyes. To make matters worse, the boss classed them as lazy buffoons.

'Go and give those fools a hand, George!' he'd say, 'or the lazy so-and-so's won't be finished until midnight ... ' – as indeed they never were. Well, that isn't quite correct. I remember the time when a cowman called Phillip got home before twelve o'clock one night . . .

Earlier that evening we were all called out to go into the wood to fell enough timber so that the boss could knock up a poultry house. Another thing he wanted in a hurry. It was late May, we got stuck in, and by dusk we had finished, except for one tall straight tree that was needed for a ridge pole; and it wasn't long before that too was felled.

Unfortunately it wouldn't come free. It was caught in the undergrowth and rested on an ash sapling which was bowed over almost to breaking point.

'I can see what's holding it,' yelled the boss in the failing light.

'There's a slither of wood not quite cut through.' With that, he swiped at it with his axe. The tree rolled free. The sapling, released from its load, came up with a woosh and struck Phillip, who was standing too close for comfort, smack in the face.

It blacked his eyes, spread-eagled his nose, rammed his pipe stem down his throat, smashing the bowl against his front teeth — splitting his lip and singeing his moustache. Phil hit the deck and lay groaning in the nettles.

'Are you all right?' asked the boss.

'What a stupid question to ask. Of course I'm all right. I'm enjoying every bloody minute of it.'

The boss, perhaps feeling he'd pushed things too far, dismissed the sarcasm and lifted Phil on to his feet to examine his wounds. He then decided, quite uncharacteristically, that as far as Phil was concerned he could call it a day. It was well past ten!

'Have an early night, Phil,' he soothed.

Phil, having collected his bits and pieces together, staggered away into the darkness, closely followed by a warning voice yelling:

'Don't be late in the morning, Phil. Remember you're on early turn!'

Late-hour Merger-thoughts

I SEE, even at this late hour, that our editor is still soliciting comment on whether or not we have anything to gain by throwing in our lot with another union, one more muscular and financially stable than our own.

Well, months, the biennial conference and the recall have passed since I had what I thought then was a final say on the matter; in the meantime quite a number of fresh thoughts on the merger have entered my head. So, as we are having a stay of execution, I'm taking the opportunity this offers to make known four of them, hoping all the while that they have the desired effect.

First: I've heard of a passenger parachuting out of a plane because he didn't like the sound of the engine, but have heard no reports of his parachuting back into it again when he discovered that he liked the look of the ground below even less.

Second: Ours is the only union that does not support a cheap food policy. In view of this, I wonder who will do the compromising, them or us?

Third: There is nothing at the moment pre-
venting those among us who think they would be
better off in some other union from joining which-
ever one it is that takes their fancy straight away.

Fourth: If the worst comes to the worst and the
union that takes us over demands we change our
picturesque badge for something plainer and more
in keeping with it's own, then let our new badge
depict a cherry — less two bites!

It would symbolize the hesitancy of those who
voted one way at Cromer and just the opposite at
the recall. A badge like that would also carry with
it my hope that the second bite turns out to be
sweeter than the first; for, as I've already said, the
decision will be irreversible.

I'll Christen my Half

AS A long-standing advocate of 'less grace and more gravy' I appreciate in full Brother Gunston's feelings towards churches and cathedrals, although I would remind him and others too who wrote to the *Landworker* in a like vein, that the gathering in St Albans on the last day in May wasn't there to celebrate but to commemorate the Peasants' Revolt, and there's quite a difference between the two.

There was a time not so long ago when I too would have fought shy of going into St Albans cathedral. The thought of having to live with my own conscience afterwards would have been a strong enough deterrent to keep me on the outside. As it was, my footsteps faltered a little on the day as we neared the cathedral's holy portals, and no doubt, had I not been accompanied by as sound a body as the old edifice has seen for many a day, I would have lost my nerve and not gone in.

Looking back on the days of my inflexible resolve to disown religion and all its trappings, I now see myself as something of a bigot — no better than a religious fanatic, in fact.

Mind you, those days weren't by any means easy days for me; for besides the soul searchings that went on inwardly as to the rights or wrongs of my unbelief, I had the external influence of tradition and cant to contend with as well. Looking around it seemed impossible to do anything of the slightest importance without first looking skyward and beseeching that a heavenly seal be set upon it.

Happily, I'm no longer a purist. What's more, I remember to the minute that time when my resolve began to crumble. It marked the end of an argument between the wife and myself over whether or

'He's half mine, and that counts for something too.'

not our son should be christened. The argument had been going on far too long when, in exasperation, my wife said:

'Why do you have to be so pig-headed about it. Why should you have all the say. He's my son as well as yours, surely that counts for something?'

'That cuts both ways,' I snapped, 'He's half mine, and that counts for something too.'

'All right then,' she countered. 'I'll allow you that, but I'm christening my half. What you do with yours is entirely up to you!'

The Farmer and the Fiddle

WE OUGHT to compile 'A Treasury of Country Humour and Tall Tales from the Land.' What a Treasury that would be! One that would enrich the bookshelves of the world with pathos and mirth. One that could become an all-time bestseller. While for us, for the first time ever, it would bring gravy galore!

Just think for one moment of all the rubies and pearls that there are scattered around the countryside waiting to be collected together, polished up, and resold as sparkling wit. Gems, for example, like the one I'm about to lay before you, which I picked up in flashes one evening as I followed close behind a couple of colleagues at the Brighton conference taking a 'leg-stretcher' along the front. Since reception was none too good, I've taken the liberty of filling in a gap or two, here and there. I hope mine is a true version. May God forgive me if it isn't!

The tale could either be called 'Fiddling in the Wind' or just plain 'Snuffin' It!'. It's about a farmworker who, quite some time ago, had forgotten to mix seed-dressing in with his seed corn, and in desperation decided to apply the dressing neat, with a fiddle, onto the land he had just drilled. (Perhaps older readers will explain to the younger ones what an agricultural fiddle is, and how it functions).

'The dressing was powerfully toxic … the wind was mischieviously high … ' said one colleague to the other, 'the ol' boy had twelve acres, roughly, to cover.'

'The wind didn't bother him then?' the other asked.

'Not at first, and then only when he faced into it. All the same, it played havoc with his aim, and blew the powder up his nose.'

'He kep' on though, did he?'

'Oh yes. He fiddled away almost till dinner-time. By then, even he, as keen as he was, could stick it no longer. A gamekeeper and his mate found him lying, along with his bike, outside a 'phone-box − spark out.

'They couldn't tell whether he had been trying to call for an ambulance or telling his wife to put his dinner in the oven. Anyway, they dialled 999 and got him into hospital.'

'Was he very ill?'

'Was he ill? I'll say he was ill! They had to change his blood more often than they changed his bed-clothes.'

'Did he recover?'

'Not really. To tell the truth, they didn't quite know what to do for him. He wasted almost to nothing; and when they couldn't find his pulse, they took his word for it that he was still alive and discharged him on the grounds that he was in danger of being slung out with the dirty laundry.'

'Did he linger on for long after that?'

'Surprisingly, he rallied for a short while; staggered to his feet, and spent most of the little time he had left loafing in the entrance hall of a Private Chapel of Rest soaking up the atmosphere, and the remainder kneeling in church praying for an increase in the funeral benefit. Alas, he was a 'gonna' within a month.'

'Was he buried — or cremated?'

'Actually, they couldn't dig a grave narrow enough to give him a snug fit, so they cremated him, and while they were at it, threw in his fiddle to make up a presentable heap of ashes. These, unfortunately, were scattered in the Garden of Remembrance, and withered the bloom on three beds of roses.'

'So, that was the end?'

'Not quite. His widow left his cap, his coat and his choker hanging in the granary; and they did to the saw-toothed grain beetle what Mrs Thatcher has done to the British economy!'

The *seed fiddle*, delightfully named because of the similarity in action to a violin or fiddle. Here the wooden bow is strung with a leather thong instead of catgut. As the bow is moved from side to side the thong passes over the base of the spreader, causing the seed from the container to be broadcast in a band about twelve feet wide. The seed was fed onto the spreader from a bag, and the rate of feed could be controlled by a small lever at the rear of the fiddle. *(Photograph courtesy of the Estate of Douglas Lawson)*

Merger

 IT WAS a plaintive tune indeed that Gardener Cattermole piped to us (Letters, November's *Landworker*) from his own forlorn and forsaken corner of what is otherwise recognised as being the 'earty, 'ealthy, 'omely, 'appy county of 'erts. He has all my sympathy. 'For who can bear to feel himself forgotten?' Let us hope, therefore, that he can comfort himself in the knowledge that the way he feels today others have felt in the past and, no doubt, countless others in the future will be feeling that they, too, are being left out of things. I know what it's like, all right. For almost a year I put in a regular appearance at the monthly meetings of a Discussion Group in a nearby town without speaking to anyone or being spoken to in return. I was gradually coming to the conclusion that they weren't really bothered about me, when suddenly the 'cat was out of the bag' and I was left in no doubt whatever that I was a rank outsider — a Brillo-pad in a box of Shredded Wheat.

The moment of truth came towards the end of a

long drawn out discussion on an item under the heading: 'The benefits set against the cost of street lighting' (Can you imagine it? And me with nothing more powerful than a flickering candle in a jam jar to lighten the darkness on the way to our 'loo' under the limes at the bottom of our garden in the sticks!) The Chairman, on bringing the group to order by rapping on his table with the edge of his spectacle case, declared: 'Ladies and Gentlemen, I'm afraid time is running out on us. I think we ought to draw this discussion to a close ... ' then pausing, he turned to me for the first time ever, nodded knowingly, and added, 'it's getting very late, and I'm sure the caretaker is waiting to lock up!'

*　　*　　*

I hope you will take care when the time comes for you to vote on the merger issue and that you won't let the fresh lick of honey which the Off-guard-and-join-'em brigade are at present smearing on the T & G bait, lure you into acting against your better judgement. I'm referring, of course, to the 'Anything we can do they can do better' benefit tables in the *Landworker* Special Merger Supplement.

There may be other reasons, which so far have escaped me, why we should merge; but the whole concept of Trade Unionism as I see it would have to be stood on its head before I would be wanting to switch from one union to another simply because there was a pound or two extra to be gained by doing so should I become incapacitated through an injury sustained at work, or because I could see in it a chance of saving myself from the final disgrace of a pauper's grave when, eventually, I keel over and bow out.

The cobbler should stick to his last. Every penny that members pay into the Union should be used fighting the good fight to see that accidents at work are kept to a minimum. More important still, to see to it that when Misfortune lays a worker low, he hasn't hitherto led such a hand-to-mouth existence, his reserves cannot even match the derisory amounts that the NUAAW (or the T&GWU, come to that!) pays out in the way of benefits in times of trouble.

Shun the honied bait! Instead, ask yourself this: Who is more likely to fight the better fight on our behalf to help bring these things about — our own people with their undivided commitment to our cause, or those people whose loyalties will have to be split between the 2 million or more crying out for cheap food on the one hand, and the 75 thousand demanding far, far higher wages for producing it on the other?

The Tykes Amen

WITH THE air of a physician burying a body he has just 'done in' by prescribing the wrong medicine over a long period of time, Ray Carey (January's Letters) gives the covering mound a last, sinister pat with the back of his shovel, then sets about the mourners for questioning whether there's a better life to come in the Hereafter.

Now, I don't want to appear ungrateful to him, after all, it was mainly through his efforts that I was able to round off my education at York University — the venue of last November's Yorkshire farm-worker's conference; for I learned there, much to my astonishment, that Ray, along with his fellow Tykes, lacks the dour, down-to-earth, matter-of-factness which we, oft thought less discerning souls from the south, have been given to understand Yorkshire folk are endowed with.

Incredible as it may seem, up there they actually believe in fairy-godmothers. They simply just can't wait until the arrival of their own particular favourite with her gift-wrapped survival kit.

Sad that!

Maddening, though, was Fred Kendall's sharp about-turn to the rostrum he'd just left, to pronounce, more by way of traditional impulse than rational thought, the Tykes' Amen: 'Contributions must not be raised.' A pronouncement which has starved our Union of funds for far longer than anyone cares to remember.

Ray complains of there not being, in all those thousands of words written in anti-merger letters, one believable recipe for survival. He's wrong there! Although one must agree it would appear unbelievable in his eyes that our survival could be secured and our independence sustained with hard cash from our own pockets.

How Big is Yours?

I CAN never understand why it is that whenever mention is made of a farmer it can never be made without coupling his name to the number of acres he owns.

It seems as though you can refer to a parson without, at the same time, letting the world know how many empty pews he is preaching to every Sunday; a deck-chair attendant, without revealing the number of finger-trapping cheap recliners he's responsible for; or a sweep, without announcing from the roof-top the soot dislodging, rod lengths he can reach to ... but not so with a farmer. Every single acre belonging to him, be it smothered with powdery mildew or strewn with mossy boulders, must be accounted for and linked with his name.

For all I know, farmers may disapprove of this peculiar habit; though, come to think of it, I can't say that I've heard any openly complain about the linkage. However, I am pretty certain that they are aware of it. This became apparent to me some years ago, when my boss, on arriving home after a tour of the American corn belt, called me over and asked (as though he didn't already know!) how many acres we were farming.

'One eighty two,' I said. 'Why do you ask?'

'Just checking, that's all,' he replied. Then in a confessional aside, he explained that on his trip back to England, he had become pally with a couple of American cereal growers — outward bound for a 'mosey around the Old Country' — and after listening to their boasting about the huge acreage they farmed, he felt compelled to add a nought or two when the question of his own acreage was put to him.

'I shouldn't sleep too fitfully over that,' I advised, 'after all, farmers are farmers the world over, and it would have been strange thing indeed if your companions from the States hadn't already added a few noughts to their own as well.'

But stay reader stay! It's important to say: there are times when farmers wax coy over the number of acres they own. Do a job for one on an acreage basis, and his fields shrink faster than a cheap suit in the rain!

Ribbons that Fade
and Cups that Gather Dust

I CAUGHT my breath and my blood ran cold as I read the Kent 'Around the Counties' report (March *Landworker*) about the off-hand attitude of farmer Hugh MacWatt towards his one-time employee, Dave Hopkins — a ploughman of distinction.

Now, don't think for one moment that there has been a change of heart on my part regarding champion ploughmen. Far from it. If anything, the report makes me want to discourage them even more.

So, what, you may ask, is so shocking about it then? Well, it's this: If farmers can treat the elite among their workers with such callousness and contempt, and get away with it — where do we lesser mortals stand?

With a whole year in which to figure things out, I would have thought the least the match ploughmen of East Kent could have done by way of protest, was to have made the venue of the event a 'No-go' area on match day.

Sadly though, all we get is an after-the-match picture in *Landworker* of our Brother holding aloft his trophies, in a spirit which can only be likened to that of a front-runner in the Obedience Class at Crufts. It certainly makes the workers' stand at Bernard Matthews look great stuff!

Tony Gould's comment in the same report does nothing to warm my chilled blood either; for he is not half as convinced about farmers not knowing their own business as I am of us not knowing ours.

Bert Hazell surprises me too. Just fancy, Bert of all people, writing in his review of 'Brother to the Ox' about ' ... the joy of handling well groomed horses with plaited tails and mains bedecked with ribbons ... and the brasses which shone till one could see oneself in them ... ' when all the handler could see reflected therein — presuming he had time for such vanities — was the image of someone who was overworked, underpaid and badly housed; whose children walked hungry and sometimes barefoot to school, to be taught little more than to know their station in life and to respect their betters.

Perhaps I'm being a little unkind. I'd forgotten that the boys were also taught how there were bright ribbons and shining pots to be won later in life, provided they shamed their mates with straighter furrows or with some other better-presented skills. What they weren't told, however, was how soon those ribbons fade, and how dull and useless cups can become.

Cuppatenosynivitis

'WOW!' HOW about that, then!' exclaimed a non-farming friend of mine as he eased himself back from the front edge of his seat at the close of the final session of the 'One Man and his Dog' televised champion sheepdog trials.

To such wild acclaim, my only reply was to admit that even the losers had more than earned their daily tickle under the chin and their occasional condition powder. However, I felt that it wouldn't be right to leave it at that, so, after making clear to him my detestation of farming competitions, I confessed that my wonderment had been taken up more by the compliant anticipations of the sheep than by the dexterity of the dogs. Every move of the sheep, from 'lift' to 'pen' had me increasingly believing in the nursery-rhyme guidance given to Bo-Peep ' . . . leave them alone, and they will come home.' (Bringing their dogs behind them?)

Knowing more about the wiles of farm animals than my friend, I suggested to him that if the trials are meant to be a test of intelligence over instinct it

would prove more were each dog to be presented
with an unruly 'gang o' five' — the champion being
the quickest dog to realise that his lot were uncontrollable and to return to heel, signalling: 'Master,
they're hopeless. That scattering of mutton-heads
would break the heart of the lovable Phil Drabble
himself.'

It is unlikely though, that trialists would warm
to my suggestion, as sound as it is. They're more
likely to search out an even more compliant breed
of sheep; one specially suitable for televised trials.
In any event, I wouldn't mention such a thing to
experts in shepherding. With them, even if they
stand to gain by what you have to say, it pays to
keep quiet. The less you pretend to know the more
they love you for it.

Take the following incident for example . . .

It took place on a country estate; a model establishment where the management boasted they had
the best of everything. Everything, that is, except
for a Kerry Hill flock on which they had lavished
all with scant reward. The blame for the flock's
poor performance had been laid on the shoulders of
the Southdown ram with whom the ewes had been
crossed; consequently, he had been given the 'chop'
and replaced by Larry, an outstanding, black-faced,
amber-eyed Suffolk — the finest ram money could
buy.

As tupping time was a few months off, it
seemed that for the time being, Larry had been
given the run of a special paddock close by the

workers' cottages just off the farm drive.

Obviously, being an employee of little standing on the estate, no one had consulted me on the change; nor, come to that, had they advised me of the newcomer's arrival or his whereabouts ... however, I was soon to find out.

We were busy silage making at the time and I had been told to take the green-crop loader (a Wilde-Thwaites) to an outlying farm. On the way, I decided to call in home for a 'quick cuppa' and, in order not to advertise the fact, parked the tractor and loader out of sight in the afore-mentioned paddock. On my return, I climbed on to the tractor, opened the throttle and pulled away.

'Bump!' ... 'Bump!'

'What the hell's that,' I thought, and on investigating discovered Larry with a lack-lustre look in

'I'd better do something to revive the poor old sod.'

his eyes, lying in the loader's tracks in the long grass — out for the count. 'That's torn it,' I said to myself, 'I'd better do something to revive the poor old sod.' So, not fancying a mouth to mouth resuscitation job, I hurried off for a bucket of water (a splash of water does marvels for battered boxers twixt rounds, you know) and on returning, much to my amazement and delight, found that Larry was up on all fours again. He took a swig from the bucket, and in no time was flicking his ears and munching the grass about his feet. Believing in miracles, a much relieved George went on his way.

Two days later, I met the head shepherd walking towards the farm office carrying a soggy mass in an opened sack.

'What's up?' I asked.

'Larry's gone,' he choked.

'What, got out?'

'Got out be buggered. He's snuffed it!'

'Snuffed it? Gawdallmighty! I wonder why?'

'Not a clue. He went so sudden. We sha'n't know till after the post mortem.'

With that, he spread the sack on the ground, showed me various bits and pieces of Larry's 'innards' and explained that he was parcelling them up and sending them off for laboratory tests at Edinburgh University.

Quite some time after that, I chanced to have a word with him about the cause of Larry's passing.

'Did you ever find out?' I asked.

'Oh, yes. He died of a disease with a name as

long as your arm.' Then, with an air of superiority, he drew a laboratory report from his jacket pocket and told me that I wouldn't understand it any more than he did.

He was wrong though. It meant 'Runoverwithagreencroploader.' But I wasn't going to tell him that. He wouldn't have appreciated my helpfulness if I had.

Shivery-shakes

A REALLY good education, in my view, teaches you to feel at ease when dealing with influential people and more importantly, makes you brass-necked enough to ask them a favour or two.

Bluff is important, too. 'Bullshit baffles brains' was the text and extent of my education in the British Army. Strange to say, I received an unasked for refresher course on 'Bluff' soon after my return to Civvy Street . . .

One day, back on the farm, finding myself on the right end of some rare praise for a job well done, I used it as a lever to try and 'up' my wages. My flatterer, an eminent figure in the farming world and the agricultural consultant to my boss, paled at my request. He wasn't there, he said, as a wage-rise consultant: nevertheless, he saw my difficulties, and as a great personal favour, offered some sound advice in lieu of a rise.

His advice was that if I wanted to get on, I should never be afraid of accepting a challenge . . . 'Even if it means bluffing your way through,' he advised. 'Say, for instance, you are walking the land with a prospective employer who, in testing your knowledge, asks you to identify a weed you know nothing of. Don't admit it. Instead, make up a likely sounding name. If he challenges it's authenticity, boldly tell him that that's what you have always called it; for that's the name it's known by in your part of the world.'

One year later in similar circumstances — I was on a month's trial — I tried cashing in on the consultant's advice. I was walking over a farm with a new boss when we came upon a clump of weeds in a field of barley that were strange to me:

'We'll have to do something about these, Scales,' he said, then paused (I assumed) to allow me time to name the weed.

'What those blasted Shivery-shakes?' I blurted out.

'*Shivery-shakes*?' he exploded. '*Shivery-shakes*?' Then he leapt into the air and came crashing down with both feet upon one of the tassle-headed weeds. 'That's a *Wild oat*, I'll have you know.'

Forgetting the full text of the advice, I replied: 'Any idiot can see it's wild now, but it looked placid enough to me before you bloody well jumped on it.'

Our relationship deteriorated from that moment on, and we parted company long before the weed cast its seeds and increased my ex-employer's stock of Shivery-shakes . . . Sorry, Wild oats.

Safety: Spot-checking

FARM SAFETY is far too important an issue to be left in the hands of spot-checkers. If we don't watch out, in our mistrustful way, we shall next be asking for spot-checkers to check on spot-checkers to see that spot-checkers are checking OK.

And anyway, what's wrong with us doing a little checking on our own account? Or is that asking too much? Wait ... I feel a poem coming on.

Who slipped that clapped out trailer down the orchard?
   Who hid that wonky ladder up the lane?
Who fixed those rusty guards, all bent and tortured,
   To pass a test ... then took them off again?
Who found that dusty box (t'was near depleted
   Of first aid salves you ought to keep in store)
And rushed to get it suddenly repleted
   To sate the prying eye — and nothing more?
Who poked those birds' nests from that dust extractor?
   Who hitched those rails around the slurry pit?
Who to his face called Safety-man a benefactor;
   Behind his back, a bloody nosey twit?
No ...

Was not your boss, his wife or son or daughter;
(And what I say is absolutely true)
     Their hands are clean of doing things they didn't 'oughter'
Those dangerous things, they leave safely up to you!

Men of Straw

AS TIME goes by, Ian Crawford will learn, as ADHACs have revealed, that very few workers want to stay on in their cottages after their employment has terminated. The cottages are mostly 'crummie' old places anyway; and the workers can't swap 'em for council houses quick enough.

We shouldn't waste our time pushing for ADHAC documentation on behalf of our members; we would do better striving to get the Ministry's report supporting the farmer's case done away with.

That said, full marks to Ian for his kind words about a decent wage for our members. Decent enough, I would say, to enable us to buy our own houses, thereby putting an end to our grovelling around for housing favours from the local council. Unfortunately, so long as we act like second class citizens, we'll be treated as such.

---

* ADHACs (Agricultural Dwelling House Advisory Committees) are the tribunals which decide whether the farmer can prove 'agricultural need' for possession of a tied cottage.

The Trust of a Child

IN THE fifties when the pick-up baler was coming into its own, it was the usual practice for the arable farmer to let the dairyman bale and take away, free of charge, the straw left lying in the cornfields behind the Combine Harvester.

As I was the 'outside' foreman on a sizeable dairy farm in those days, my involvement in this 'straw-up-for-grabs' exercise was quite considerable. It had me baling, almost non-stop, seven days a week right through corn harvest and beyond. A boring overlong season which I thought might be shortened if the boss replaced the mate I had (a pensioner, well past the job's demands) with someone whose appetite for work hadn't been dulled by a lifetime's heavy toil.

I mentioned this to him one evening after a particularly frustrating day, and he asked me if I knew of anyone.

'Yes,' I replied, 'young Jimmy Simms.* Although he's only a schoolboy, by what I've seen of him, he'd cope quite easily with the work. There is

just one snag, he's been helping Mr Hogg*
(another farmer) since the summer holidays began
and may need a little enticing to come. Still, that
shouldn't be too difficult, Hogg's a poor payer,
anyway. I'll tell Jimmy that he'll be getting a man's
pay for doing a man's job . . . all right?' The boss, a
man hungry for straw, half nodded in assent: and
before he had time to change his mind, I was at the
lad's house putting the proposition to him.

Jimmy was taken aback by the offer almost to
the point of disbelief. Then, to reassure him, I said:
'Look, tomorrow's Wednesday. If you come baling with me, stick at it and do a good job, I'll see to
it, come Friday night, you'll be five pounds better
off. To hell with Hogg.' Within seconds the boy's
doubt turned to exuberance and he eagerly asked:
'What time do I start?'

'Eight, sharp.'

'I'll be there.'

And he was, too; and right from the word 'go' I
could see that I hadn't over-estimated his capabili-
ties. Throughout the day, he impatiently tugged
those bales from the machine, loaded them on the
sledge, then slid them off on to the stubble stacked
in sixteens, leaving them there, rank on rank, as
straight as Guardsmen on parade. Besides that, he
constantly informed me of our progress, all the
while assuring me that I could go faster yet.

Moving at an unheard-of rate, the baler fair

---

* The names Jimmy Simms and Mr Hogg are fictitious.

Cutting rye

gobbled up the straw; field after field of it until, by late Friday afternoon, we found ourselves working directly in the wake of the Harvester. We had caught up. 'That's it Jimmy,' I said. 'Let's call it a day and go and draw our earnings.' His face lit up.

As we reached my cottage gate, on the way to the farm, I told him to go on without me as I wanted to tell my wife that we had finished earlier than usual. No longer steadied now by my easy walk, the lad rushed off. I followed on shortly after only to meet him coming back from the farm, in tears.

'What's the matter Jimmy?'

'I'm not telling you,' he sobbed. 'I'm never gonna speak to you ever again. Never!' And he struck out at me with his dinner bag, then he hared for home.

Nonplussed, and with his cry of 'cheat-cheat-cheat' ringing in my ears, I continued on to the farm where I met the boss — breathing heavier than usual.

'What's Jimmy so upset about?' I asked.

'I'll give him upset. That, I will! Coming here demanding two weeks' pay for half a week's work. Whatever next? When I've sorted out his proper rate he'll get all he's entitled to. That, and no more.'

'There's only one "proper rate", and that,' I angrily reminded him, 'we sorted out on Tuesday evening. You've welshed on him! But I won't. I'll see that he gets all that he's been promised. Even if it means paying him myself.'

'You do *just* that. Here's your money. Goodnight.'

I was soon back at Jimmy's place asking his mother if I could have a word with him. After much coaxing he came to the door and stood there — work-soiled, tear-stained and shattered.

'I've brought your money,' I said, forcing a smile.

'That's yours, not mine. You'll not get round me that easy.'

'Come on Jimmy, be sensible. You worked hard for it. Do me a favour — take it.'

'You do me one — clear off!'

Too proud to throw my own hard earned money at the hapless lad's feet, in sadness I turned and walked away. I had lost something precious and irretrievable: The trust of a child. And for what?

Free bedding straw, and a meanness that goes back to biblical times.

Spuds for Haircuts

 I WAS interested in Brother Tabiner's comparison at Westminster when he was talking in terms of haircuts, and said that his wages bought him more 'trim-ups' before the war than his wages do now.

In the twenties my father supplemented his meagre farm pay by cutting hair, and he had to cut fourteen heads for enough money to buy a sack of spuds. Today, my barber (the cheapest in town) earns a sack in three. Someone's got ahead, but it hasn't been the likes of Cyril and me!

Working for the Kindling

FOR THE best part of my working life, I was under the mistaken impression that when it came to negotiating terms, I was supreme; and there was nothing the Union could do on a collective basis that I couldn't do better by acting on my own account. It is easy to see now why my bosses gave me every encouragement to keep thinking that way.

'You drive a hard bargain, Scales,' they used to say. 'You don't need to be in a union. You can work things out all right on your own. You don't need a stick to get around on.'

And while they were buttering me up, they must have been thinking how wonderfully accommodating I was. If they hadn't been thinking like that, they would never have tried certain things on and got away with them in the way they did.

Just one incident from the many that come to mind clearly illustrates the point I'm making.

There once was a field of kale which needed thinning, and I was given the responsibility of seeing that the work was done.

To this end, I found several casual workers and set them thinning out on an agreement with my boss that they would be getting paid a certain amount for the first twenty rows each man thinned a day and, in order to keep the men sweet and the job moving, a little extra for each row thinned above 20. Meanwhile, for my part, I agreed to hoe along with them for my normal pay and the promise that when the job was completed I could have a useful portable garden shed belonging to the farmer, for which I had been asking for quite some time.

The job progressed well and was soon out of the way. The hoers departed, quite happy with things. Me too, I'd worked the oracle, and the garden shed was mine.

But wait. Fate was in a spoiling mood.

Because I had neither the time nor the transport, I was unable to shift the shed straight away, so it

'Seems you're out of luck,' observed my boss

had to be left, for the time being, standing under a massive elm. Sad to say, the wind got up in the night and sent one of the largest boughs on the elm crashing down on to my shed.

'Seems you're out of luck,' observed my boss the next morning, as together we viewed the wreck.

'Yes,' I replied, 'and it seems I'm the only worker you'll find for miles around who, over the past fortnight, has been hoeing away like fury for a heap of kindling wood.'

Bumpkins who Buffered
the Bosses

JIM WAS one of that great band of farm labourers, assumed to be dim-witted, who was quite the reverse in actual fact. Measuring tapes meant little to him; he preferred his own more flexible ways of workings things out.

Jim was with me, helping at the back of an old Smythe drill, on the day that I was first sent to sow a field with corn. The field was of irregular shape and size; the seed expensive and in short supply. Getting it all on evenly all over would have set an experienced drillsman a stiff test. To a novice like me, it presented an overwhelming proposition.

Little wonder then, that towards the end of such an exasperating day, after trying to work out for the umpteenth time the position regarding the acreage yet to be drilled and the right cog to be using, the answer seemed to be as remote as ever. So, in desperation, I turned to Jim, who was no stranger to the old Smythe or the field, and asked him if there were any signs that I should be looking for which would show me whether the seed was going on correctly or not.

'See that holly,' he said, as he pointed to a lone tree growing in the hedgerow about two-thirds of the way along the headland. 'Well, if you're worrying yourself silly about not having enough before getting to it, and fretting about having too much left over after passing it, you'll be all right. This field's that cussed sort of shape.'

Who, among today's technocrats, could have put it more reassuringly than that? Yesterday's farm labourers may be seen as bumpkins, but bumpkins they never were.

Teardrops and Peardrops

 MRS THATCHER has her own cheeky, winning way of disposing of council houses. She hands people doles from their own store; and for that their gratitude knows no bounds. She reminds me of a certain Nancy Puke, a farmer's wife whose contemptuous ways have been exposed before in these pages. This anecdote well illustrates their similarity:

In the 20s when, to a working-class child, a halfpenny represented a small fortune and a penny was riches indeed, an unusually thrifty play-mate of mine went into our village shop with a penny, bought a ha'p'orth of sweets and came out clutching her purchase in one hand and her halfpenny change in the other. On her way home she dropped the coin and lost it in the long grass, whereupon she began to cry.

Mrs Puke, passing by, noticed the child's distress and asked her why she was crying. The girl sobbed out her sad story. 'Dear dear,' soothed the farmer's wife. 'You mustn't cry.' With that, she opened the child's bag of sweets, selected a pear-drop and popped it into the girl's mouth, saying: 'There now. Here's a sweetie for you. That should make you forget that nasty little halfpenny.'

See now what I mean about Maggie? I hope so.

'There now. Here's a sweetie for you.'

What ADHACs are About

I'D LIKE to retell a few words spoken at an ADHAC hearing this year.

Things were running quite smoothly (they usually do when the farmer and his ex-worker agree to be questioned together by the committee); so smoothly, in fact, that the worker, no doubt misled by the seeming chumminess of the proceedings, took exception to a pertinent question we were putting to his ex-boss, and brazenly asked:

'I wish someone would tell me what these bloody ADHACs are all about, anyway.'

There was an embarrassed silence. No one spoke.

So, seeing as the others were disinclined to tell him, I thought that I had better enlighten him.

'If the chairman won't tell you,' I began, 'and my farmer colleague on the right won't either, I will. If the farmworkers' union hadn't persisted in its endeavour to get the Act on the statute book, you wouldn't be sitting here beside your old boss supporting him in his claim. By now he would have taken you to court like a common criminal, and had you evicted no matter whether you had somewhere else to go to or not.

'That's what the ADHACs are all about, brother . . . as simple as that!'

An Egg for a Leg

 I'LL NOT join in the 'pinching or perks' controversy which surfaced on page three of last month's *Landworker*; only remind the reader that the appropriation of unauthorised perks — thought to be quite justifiable on the ox-that-treads-the-corn principle — can sometimes have far-reaching consequences involving the innocent in a manner out of all proportion to the original 'crime', as I can illustrate as follows.

Shell shocked!

Towards the end of the First World War, when thousands of survivors were limping homeward, hoping to pick up the threads of the quieter life they once knew, my father was transferred into the General Service Corps and drafted to work on the land. He had been wounded: physically and mentally. His nerves, in particular, were in a shocking state. The three-year stress of a front-line existence had taken its toll and left him with a vile, uncontrollable temper.

A fellow draftee was already establishing himself on the same farm when dad arrived there. Unlike dad, he had lost a leg; but his nerves were sound, and so was his sense of survival — a useful thing to keep intact when there's famine in the land, as there was in Britain in 1917. He had taken over the gamekeeping, a job of trust with considerable latitude. My father was left with the stockman's duties which, among other things, entailed milking the two house-cows.

It was discovered, shortly after the two draftees arrived, that some of the barnyard fowls weren't using the padlocked nest-boxes. Eggs were missing! This, for the farmer's family in a time of shortage, was calamity far worse than the war itself. They suspected that the new stockman was enticing the hens into the cowshed to lay. But they were on the wrong track.

One afternoon the farmer's wife was on the prowl trying to catch the culprit, when (in my father's words) this is what happened ...

'She came sidling into the cowshed just as I was about to start milking. She hadn't noticed me there, down on the stool. She cast her eyes suspiciously over every possible nesting site, then gingerly worked her way to where my greatcoat hung and lightly brushed the pockets with the back of her hand. Surprised at finding them empty, she turned her attention to the sleeves and began to examine them for any egg-shaped irregularities ... but I cut her examination short.

'I was raving mad. I leapt from the stool, kicked it to one side, rushed across to my coat, grabbed it and beat it on the floor. First one side then the other; time and time again. Then I threw it down, stamped on it, kicked it about the cowshed and, after all that, picked it up and held it up in front of the snooper.

"Come on, you snipe-nose interloper," I bellowed. "Push your hands into these pockets, and if you haven't got the makings of an outsized omelette on them when you pull them out, I'll be wanting an apology from you!" But did she apologise? Did she hell. She turned tail, rushed off and reported me to the boss.

'He was soon on the scene. "I won't tolerate such disgraceful behaviour," he said, with hurt importance. "Get this into your head, my man. You are not so disabled you can't bear arms again for your King and country in their hour of need. I'll have you sent back into the trenches. Meanwhile, not another word from you, or you'll be in real trouble."

'Just imagine, all that upset over a measly, half dozen eggs. Need you ask who was taking them? The game keeper, of course. He used to show them to me as he plopped them, one by one, out of sight into the daily can of milk he was allowed for his ferrets. He'd tap his wooden leg, wink an eye, and say: "An egg for a leg. A fair exchange, eh? You should take your share too — they're good for the nerves!"

Greenham and Grenada

THERE MIGHT be a good reason for my feeling more hopeful, and justified in expecting a favourable response from the Russians, if we began showing them a sign of why they should trust us rather than increasing, to a point of lunacy, the signs of why they shouldn't.

Mind you, if they did warm to such a friendly gesture, it wouldn't necessarily mean that my worries about the future were over. The Americans would see to that. For I can't see them standing idly by while we fraternise with the 'enemy'. It's worth remembering, too, that when they take it into their minds to free us of the wayward politicians who had led us from the path of righteousness, they'll be better placed for the operation than they were when they decided to free the Grenadians of theirs.

Those gum-chewing angels of mercy wouldn't have to drop out of the sky on to us. They are here already. Feet firmly planted on the ground. Handsomely provided for; well protected; and placed outside the law!

Straw Burning

BALING UP straw behind a combine harvester is not the most glamorous of jobs. It's dusty, dirty, noisy and has a well above average share of worries attached to it.

A baler that hasn't been expertly maintained, even one with only a season's hard use behind it, can be a very temperamental tool indeed. Worn knotters, for example, can do the strangest things with a length of twine. Timing can become erratic. Tines, too, can very often pick up more trouble than loose straw. And of course, straw itself: I've seen the best of pals falling out over the uneven way in which it has been left lying in the field.

Baling is something that sane drivers fight shy of, and drivers who haven't got blue eyes, get landed with. It has even been known for the job to be foisted upon a luckless casual worker!

Take together the lack of enthusiasm for baling, carting and stacking bales, the increase in cereal acreage and the drop in demand for straw, and you'll see why Swan Vestas have become so popular with farming folk as a post-harvest aid.

Shortest Length of Union Service

I'LL NOT contest Bert Mellow's wonderful record of 47 years continuous service as a branch secretary. I'm after another. The shortest length of union service. How's this for brevity:

As a youth in the thirties, I joined the Constructional Engineers' Union one Thursday evening, and the next morning was pulled up sharp on my way to my work-place by my father, who had chased the length of the work's yard, yelling : 'Put that horrible card away out of sight you stupid little bugger ... waving it about like the ace of trumps, you'll get us both the bloody sack!'

Dad was half right. I was sacked that night. But he wasn't. He carried on working there for many years after that. I joined the Army. Thus spoiling my chance of ever winning a union long-service award; unless, of course, I live to be one hundred and ten.

Grass Roots

IF THERE is anything that infuriates me more than hearing an audience laughing only because it thinks it ought to laugh, it is hearing working people with wit enough to join a union, and maybe the Labour Party as well, being referred to as grassroot membership. Or worse still, as members at grass-root level.

I simply can't bear the thought of people I greatly admire being likened to grass. A shallow rooted plant which gets trampled over, excreted upon, chewed up, and is all too easily turfed out. As for grassroot level, with its connotations of an underworld where all things creep and crawl, could anything be more insulting than that?

Thus, having made known my objections to that belittling cliche, you'll understad why I find its perpetuation in the name of 'one of the smartest newletters yet' (that of the Southdown branch in West Sussex) so upsetting.

One would have thought that, living as they do in such a lovely part of the land, our Southdown colleagues would be inspired to give their newsletter a better name. But there it is, I suppose it could be said that any newsletter, even one with a name like 'Grassroots', is better than no newsletter at all.

In any case, we in Essex have little room to criticise. Ours died before it was christened. Perhaps more for the want of nourishment than a name. None the less, that doesn't alter the fact that I spent many a sleepless night savouring the prize money (£5 for the best title) while pondering a name for our ailing infant. But all in vain. And so it was, at a very tender age, our brainchild gave up the ghost. Nameless, it lies in unhallowed ground.

Makeshift Pins

 A PLOUGHMAN I knew, in a hurry one day, used a six-inch nail in place of a lynch pin in the cross shaft of a plough. He secured it by hammering it over at right angles.

During the course of the day the tractor lift arm worked itself partway over the head, clamping the nail between the ball-joint and the cross-shaft, with the nail jutting outwards — bayonet fashion.

As the day wore on, the man quite forgot the nail; and it was not until he was forced to leave the tractor seat to clear a blockage that he got a stabbing reminder that the nail was still firmly in place.

It left its mark on him all right! In more ways than one. He'd never use a nail again after that. No fear! Not even to hang his hat on.

There was another incident I recall where a small pin would have saved a big headache. That was harvest time, 1966, when a pre-college student was working with me, carting corn away from the combine. He seemed to me to be coping quite well. Load after load. Right up to the moment I looked down and saw him drawing alongside — trailerless, and vigorously rubbing the back of his head.

'Wherc's your trailer?' I shouted.

'It's come off!'

'How?'

'If you stop I'll tell you . . . '

'I was going fast over a bump when the drawbar pin jumped out. I didn't realise anything untoward had happened until this hosepipe arrangement (here he waved the tractor-end of the hydraulic connector pipe in my direction) after stretching to its limit, snapped, whipped back and caught me a wallop on the head.'

'Why didn't you use a lynch pin to stop the drawbar pin from jumping out?'

'I didn't think it was necessary.'

'But you think differently now, do you?'

'I'll say so,' he exclaimed, as he checked his palms for signs of blood.

Fortunately for him, no lasting harm was done. In fact, I think it did him a bit of good. It may have knocked some sense into him, because when his college days were done, he decided to sell to farmers rather than work for one. He became a rep. There's more money in that, he said. Much more!

Wanting a Bike

WHEN I was a boy I wanted a bike. My, oh my, how I wanted a bike. Not, as I reminded God each night as I knelt to pray, for joy riding or to show off on, like the nasty little swank next door, but for nobler ends. Mine would be put to the service of others, in His name. With improved mobility, what scope there would be for me to extend my mission of bringing comfort to the sick in heart.

'Dear God. Whose wisdom passeth all understanding,' I would beseech the Almighty at night before making my last 'amen'. 'Surely you can see the justice and sense in my having a bike?'

However, much to my annoyance, nothing came of it. It would seem, according to Him, there was scope enough on foot!

But that was long ago, and after recovering from the initial shock of learning that Heaven isn't a bicycle shop, I resigned myself to the divine decision; thinking I'd experienced the ultimate in heartless renouncement. I hadn't reckoned with the farmers, though, who I soon discovered, not only had the cheek of the Devil but were more stringent with pay than the Almighty is with his bicycles.

Overtime

I HAVE never been able to understand why, when I was in work, my employer was always willing to pay me more for my service at the end of the day when I was jaded and bored to distraction with the job in hand, than he was at the start when I was perky and rearing to go.

Logic tells me that if performance counts for anything at all, wages should be paid on a diminishing, rather than on an increasing scale. Making quite certain, of course, that the start rate is set high enough to ensure that the worker is content to be on his way home at a civilised hour; while his boss, knowing he has had the best out of him for the day, would be pleased to see him depart.

A scale such as that, would take the shine off overtime at a stroke. Only a fool would work longer and longer for less and less.

You must agree that it would be wonderful to hear a farmer telling his workers to knock-off at five, as he didn't feel like paying out for any more work that day — not even at the cheap rate.

CAUTION.

WHEREAS it has been represented to us from several quarters, that mischievous and designing Persons have been for some time past, endeavouring to induce, and have induced; many Labourers in various Parishes in this County, to attend Meetings, and to enter into Illegal Societies or Unions, to which they bind themselves by unlawful oaths, administered secretly by Persons concealed, who artfully deceive the ignorant and unwary,—WE, the undersigned Justices think it our duty to give this PUBLIC NOTICE and CAUTION, that all Persons may know the danger they incur by entering into such Societies.

ANY PERSON who shall become a Member of such a Society, or take any Oath, or assent to any Test or Declaration not authorized by Law—

Any Person who shall administer, or be present at, or consenting to the administering or taking any Unlawful Oath, or who shall cause such Oath to be administered, although not actually present at the time—

Any Person who shall not reveal or discover any Illegal Oath which may have been administered, or any Illegal Act done or to be done—

Any Person who shall induce, or endeavour to persuade any other Person to become a Member of such Societies,

WILL BECOME

Guilty of Felony,

AND BE LIABLE TO BE

Transported for Seven Years.

ANY PERSON who shall be compelled to take such an Oath, unless he shall declare the same within four days, together with the whole of what he shall know touching the same, will be liable to the same Penalty.

Any Person who shall directly or indirectly maintain correspondence or intercourse with such Society, will be deemed Guilty of an Unlawful Combination and Confederacy, and on Conviction before one Justice, on the Oath of one Witness, be liable to a Penalty of TWENTY POUNDS, or to be committed to the Common Gaol or House of Correction, for THREE CALENDAR MONTHS; or if proceeded against by Indictment, may be CONVICTED OF FELONY, and be TRANSPORTED FOR SEVEN YEARS.

Any Person who shall knowingly permit any Meeting of any such Society to be held in any House, Building, or other Place, shall for the first offence be liable to the Penalty of FIVE POUNDS; and for every other offence committed after Conviction, be deemed Guilty of such Unlawful Combination and Confederacy, and on Conviction before one Justice, on the Oath of one Witness, be liable to a Penalty of TWENTY POUNDS, or to Commitment to the Common Gaol or House of Correction, FOR THREE CALENDAR MONTHS; or if proceeded against by Indictment may be

CONVICTED OF FELONY,
And Transported for SEVEN YEARS.

COUNTY OF DORSET.	C. B. WOLLASTON,	HENRY FRAMPTON,
Dorchester Division.	JAMES FRAMPTON,	RICHD. TUCKER STEWARD,
	WILLIAM ENGLAND,	WILLIAM R. CHURCHILL,
February 22d. 1834.	THOS. DADE,	AUGUSTUS FOSTER.
	JNO. MORTON COLSON,	

Tolpuddle

WHEN WEIGHING up any event of the past it pays to set it in the general context of attitudes prevailing at the time. In the case of the Tolpuddle Martyrs, it must be remembered that, because of events across the English Channel, the ruling class feared for its aristocratic neck, and saw to it that any sign of suchlike revolt here was discouraged in the severest fashion.

In the light of which, the courage of those Dorsetshire labourers not only evokes admiration but marks their desperation as well. Yet, in the circumstance, desperate as it was, courage in itself was never enough to achieve the end they desired. Discretion, in fair measure, was needed too. Alas, in those fateful days leading up to their arrest, they seemed to be woefully lacking in this respect.

In fairness, though, I suppose it could be put down to their own innocence. After all, they were only labouring men unused to asserting themselves. Also, being religious men, they mistakenly thought that Right would come their way because it was right that it should.

But they were wrong.

That is why, when I step into the coach, rally bound for Tolpuddle on the great day that commemorates their 150th anniversary, I shall be taking on board with me an irreverent thought or two about the martyrs, which some people might liken to that of a Christian waking on Christmas morn, pondering the virgin birth and the immaculate conception.

I shall be asking myself: Did the Tolpuddle martyrs jump or were they pushed? Or were they just sucked in? Did they see themselves as martyrs to a cause, or mere victims of circumstance? Were they plainly bewildered by it all? Fruit ripe for the picking by both sides for completely opposite reasons in the class struggle that was simmering away and likely to boil over at any moment.

Further to that, I shall be considering where I would have fitted into the scheme of things had I been around — a farm labourer trying to improve my awful lot — living in Tolpuddle at the time. At the moment I can't see myself fitting in well at all. Especially with the antics going on at the local branch of the Friendly Society of Agricultural Labourers.

I feel that had it been left to me, there wouldn't have been any martyrs to commemorate today. Assuming, of course, that Lord Melbourne had no other shackling trickeries of Law hidden up his sumptuously brocaded sleeve. Perhaps he had!

None the less, he wouldn't have got the 'six'

seven years transportation on the strength of their contravening one of the six Acts of 1819 which prohibited 'unlawful oaths'; for the simple reason I don't believe in oaths. Lawful or otherwise.

It was in this cottage, the home of Thomas Standfield, that the men met to form the Friendly Society of Agricultural Labourers

Oaths are loathsome things — founded on fear. Oaths are wasted on the corruptible; and unnecessary in the transactions of honest men.

Consequently, I would have told James Loveless to leave his white surplice in the vestry. To ditch the blindfolds and the frightening life-size figure of a skeleton into the Piddle. To waive the ritual of initiation. As for the oaths: to shun them like the plague they are.

'Forget the mumbo-jumbo and the hocus pocus,' I would have said. 'Let's gather around us comrades who we can trust, and get down to the truly difficult business of seeing how together we

107

can best achieve the aims that we can't possibly achieve alone.'

Yes, and those gallant men would have been there in full strength; putting their heads together, devising ways of outsmarting the tyrants of church and state and the judiciary who lorded it over them. Not, as it turned out a few days later, with the branch in disarray, its members shattered and scattered. Its six best men suffering the constraints, the uncertainties and the indignities of being unceremoniously shackled and shipped off to the Antipodes. While the creeps of the establishment congratulated each other on getting yet another rigged pushover out of the way.

Except for the part they play as rallying symbols, dead heroes and suffering martyrs are spent forces. Bringing joy to those who would have it that way; and black despair in the hearts of those who crave their leadership.

Finally, a certain sadness fills me when I contemplate the years that followed the martyrs' return to England. They took no further part in establishing the trade union movement. Instead, five of them became farmers in their own right. Settling here in West Essex. Here again, there's room for regret; for they left behind them no tradition of a better paid farmworker. Farmworkers in this part of Essex are just as poorly paid as they are anywhere else.

Horseshoes for Luck

WHEN, AS a little lad I was walking one day beside an old ploughman busy with his work, I chanced to see a horseshoe lying in the furrow bottom. I stopped, picked it up, ritualistically spat on it, shut my eyes, and threw it away over my left shoulder. Then ran to catch up. 'Do you believe that horseshoes bring you luck, Mr Mundy?' I asked.

'Well boy,' he said, 'I once knew a horse which was kept on thin corn, whipped daily and worked till he dropped. He had four. And I wouldn't say that they brought that poor old beggar a lot of luck.'

'*. . . whipped daily and worked till he dropped.*'

Pushing his Luck

FARM ACCIDENTS aren't some-thing entirely new. They have been around for a long time, probably dating back to the day when man first began using sharpened tools and breaking animals to serve his will. Accidents certainly abounded in my grandfather's day. And if he is to be believed, some of them were just as horrifying as those which blood-lusting television camera crews love to zoom in on nowadays.

Like the accident concerning an angry farmer, a field of sodden hay and a vengeful god which, to his dying day, my grandfather (John Hawkins, 1857–1944) seldom ceased to talk about . . .

'From the day the field was first mown for hay late in May, until the day of the tragic happening early in July,' grandad was fond to tell, 'the rain had bucketed down without respite. And on that fateful day, for the umpteenth time, the farmer had splashed his way into the field to mourn his loss, to bemoan his lot, and to curse his Creator. Yet still it rained, as heavy as ever; while thunder rumbled all around.

'Dredging up a forkful of rotting hay from a stagnant pool, the tormented man held it to the sullen sky, and cried out: "Call yourself a loving God? What sort of hay is this? You! You couldn't make dung!"

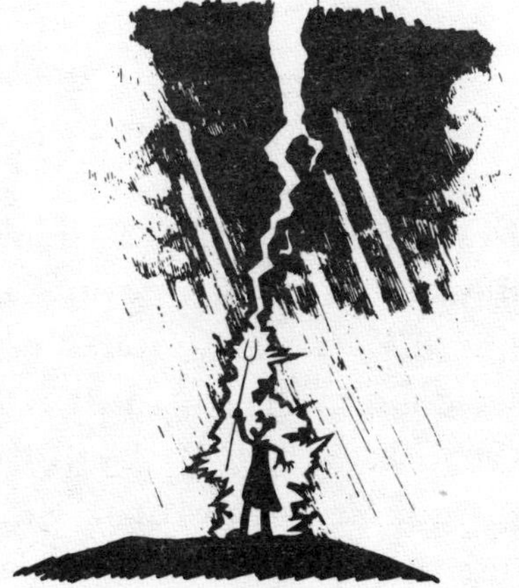

'You! You couldn't make dung!'

'That did it! There came a blinding flash and a deafening crash . . . and all that those who sought the luckless blasphemer could find when calm returned to the flooded field was a charred fork, some toasted hay, the boots the victim had been standing in, his watch stopped at three, and his ashes — barely sufficient to fill a snuffbox — floating upon the waters.'

True or not, my grandfather's grim story, which I first heard at a very impressionable age, taught me more than just to be careful in what I said and where I pointed a pitchfork in a thunderstorm. It also taught me not to tempt Providence too far — no matter the weather or the annoyance.

The Ejector Rostrum

I'D LIKE to inject a thought or two into the discussion on ways of removing a speaker who overstays his welcome at the rostrum.

Seeing as my earlier remote controlled trapdoor idea ran into some difficulties with the authorities responsible for the main drains, I am hoping that my latest invention will be more warmly received.

My Mark 2 model is based on the principle that the speaker who insists on lingering at the lectern, yawningly talking out of the back of his neck, should be helped into a better position to do so. One touch on the control switch, and the new rostrum turns 180 degrees. And if that's not enough, another touch and it will continue to rotate at ever increasing speed until the tortured waffler takes the hint and leaps off!

Stingy Boss

 TO CALL my first farmer/boss stingy, would be like calling the Atlantic a duck pond. A blood transfusion meant the same to him as it did a vampire.

He took me on as a trainee farm labourer just after the war under the government's Ex-Servicemen's Rehabilitation Scheme. (A forerunner of the YTS, or something similar). For his public spirited concern for a returning hero, he was rewarded with my labour — free. Although, it ought to be said, he was expected to pay for any overtime I worked. An arrangement which stirred him into seeing to it that I was off his land sharp at five every night.

There came a night, though, when he turned up to see me off but thought better of it. A lorry, that should have arrived earlier but had been delayed, was parked in the lane close by the clamp where a gang of us had been riddling spuds all day. It was waiting to be loaded. The rest of the gang, being smarter than me, had heard it coming, checked the time, and sloped off faster than you can say Spitalfield Market.

My boss didn't seem at all perturbed by this timely drift from the land. He quickly sized up the situation: 'You'd better stay a little while longer to help me load,' he instructed. Then, without further to-do, grabbed the 'easy' end of a loading stick and hoisted a hundredweight sack of potatoes on to my back, shouting, 'Away with it then! Don't hang about. The driver wants to get finished. He's late enough as it is.'

Quavering a little at the knees under the weight, I began loading. Sack after sack. Out of the field, through a gap in the hedge, across a ditch, over a bank, up a plank and onto the lorry. To and fro, and up and down. Again, again and again. A hundred and forty times, till the driver said, 'That's the one, mate,' and the boss told me to knock off. 'You'd better go. I'll help the driver sheet up. You're costing me a fortune,' he whined.

At dinnertime the following Friday, as I was sitting down having a bite to eat on the far side of the same field, he pulled up in his car right beside that well-trodden gap in the hedge, and beckoned me over. None too pleased at being disturbed, I trudged well over a quarter of a mile across the field to see what it was he wanted.

He handed me a lighter than light pay packet. I opened it and found a 'tanner' (2.5p) nestling in one corner.

'What's all *this* for, Guv'nor?' I asked.

'It's for helping me load those potatoes the other night, Scales. I don't want you to get the idea in

your head that I'm as mean as I'm made out to be.
Now, put it away somewhere safe, and hurry back
or you'll miss your dinner.'

Mick, Kip and Mandy

THE DOG licence should be scrapped. Dogs should be kept well fed, well groomed, well exercised and well under control – or not at all. And when it comes to dogs, I know exactly what I'm talking about, notwithstanding, it's in the same light as the old woman who said: 'I know all about children; I've buried seven.'

There have been five dogs in my life; and five's enough for me. Leaving aside the funk (the dog scared of mice) and the sheep savager (obviously!), I'll tell you a little about the other three. Mick (1936–38) first of all.

I picked him up as a reject pup, dirt cheap, at a closing-down sale about three minutes before the bankrupt proprietor shut up shop for the last time. Mick was far too young to be deprived of a mother. But as is the way in such things, he had no say in it at all. I carried him home in a shoe box, set him down on the copper – the warmest place in our house on a Saturday night – and introduced him to the rest of the family. It was only after they had gone and taken their unkind remarks with them, that it dawned on me I knew as much about dogs as they did of me.

The poor little mite yelped, whined and whimpered for his mum, with little respite, for the next six weeks. I was soon told what would happen to me as well as the 'flea-bitten wretch' if I didn't shut it up or get it out of earshot. And that explains why he came to be reared in deep straw, on Quaker Oats and condensed milk, in the shed at the bottom of our garden.

At the appropriate time, Mick weaned himself off porridge, went over to slightly underdone meat, and touched nothing else up to the end. He made little growth. Just hardened off, so to speak. But for all that, was, pound for pound, when in his prime, the most powerful beast that ever lived. Only Brunel at his best could have devised an anchorage firm enough to hold him. My mother certainly couldn't keep him in check, for all her sixteen stone.

She discovered this one Sunday evening as she prepared to set out with him to visit our uncle on the other side of the village, and was in the middle of telling us how much she was looking forward to the church service on his new wireless (we hadn't a set of our own), when she was snatched away and disappeared into the night.

She was soon back home again, though, still on tow, a well-stretched lead length behind Mick.

'How's Uncle George?' we inquired. 'I don't know,' she gasped. 'We overshot his place each time we whirled around the village. I just didn't have time to shout out and ask.'

Our move from open country into town didn't suit Mick one bit. It soured his soul. He became morose, mean tempered, ferocious and beyond control. He was forever getting me into trouble. In the end, a friend found a home for him way out in the 'sticks' with a dear old lady who, he said, had a way with dogs. She didn't have her way with Mick, though. He went straight for her throat. My friend shot him down in mid-air. Then set about reviving the terrified woman, who had passed out with fright.

Twenty years and two dogs later, Kip (1956-58) came into my life. He belonged to my son, really. A present from a distant relation. Kip was the sort of dog that had to be looked at for quite some time before one could decide which end was which. I searched both ends for his brains, but without success. A sillier terrier there could never have been. Not that Kip was aware of this. He was far too busy begetting illicit offspring to have had time for self-examination.

Centred on Stevenage, his service area covered all North Herts and spilled over into Cambridge-shire. A lorry driver also reported seeing him sniffing the Essex air on the east bank of the Stort a mile or so from Stansted.

Alas, poor Kip overstepped the mark the day he

took my boss's pampered pet on a courtship frolic in a slurry pit, then clambered out and spun-dried his shaggy coat over two horrified lady visitors the boss was escorting around the farm. The crime was unpardonable; sentence passed, and duly executed.

My son stayed with his Nan until the ghastly business was over with. All Kip's belongings were disposed of; all except his lead which, perchance, we overlooked. And, as would be expected, it was the first thing my boy noticed to remind him of his dog on his return home.

'Where's Kip?' he asked. 'Gone to Jesus,' replied my wife. 'Didn't Jesus want the lead, then?' 'No, son. Doggies don't go walkies in Heaven, the angels fasten them on long strings and fly them like kites,' I offered.

'She'd drool away the hours thinking about it.'

Queenly, is the word that best describes my last canine pal, Mandy (1964–75), although it does scant justice to her rare intelligence. Obviously, she couldn't talk; but she'd watch me out the corner of her eye whenever I was filling in a crossword puzzle, and show concern for my own intellect if I got stuck for a word.

Mandy had one vice: Chocolate! She'd drool away the hours thinking about it. The favours she would have bestowed on Kip for an After Eight mint do not bear thinking about! The day we had Mandy put to sleep (she had lung cancer) was one of the saddest days of my life, I gave her a bar of dairy milk chocolate while waiting for the vet. She looked at me knowingly. It was still there on the lawn after the vet had gone.

Yes, as I've already said, when it comes to dogs, I know what I'm talking about. And were you to offer me the pick of Crufts, I'd turn it down — even if my very best friend promised to pay the licence fee.

Love's Labours Lost

THE MAN I worked for the longest was very rich and kept pigs. The trouble with him, though, was that he couldn't keep pigmen. They were in and out of his farm like airliners in and out of Heathrow. Between-whiles, it fell to me to keep things on the move.

One Sunday morning while awaiting yet another touch down, the boss (a man who knew so little about pigs he couldn't recognise the smell) decided that, as we seemed to have more sows than rearers on the place we had better take a look at the breeding side of the enterprise to see if there were any signs of things brightening up in the future. In all probability, we were running a herd of 40–50 barreners. All as fat as the proverbial mole and as likely to pig-down as to roost in the rafters.

We walked into the sowyard, and stood together for a while listening to an occasional grunt or sigh of contentment coming up here and there from under the gently rising and falling mounds of fresh clean straw that littered the yard. Then, pointing at a great fat slob of a sow, the boss instructed me to get it on its feet. 'She must be due. It's ages since she saw the inside of the farrowing house.' he said.

I got her up. The boss looked first at her, then at me, then asked, 'Well, is she or isn't she in pig, then?' 'She is definitely not.' 'And why not?' he felt cause to ask. 'Because she is too ruddy fat,' I offered. 'Try that one. Her over there,' he continued. So, she too was made to stand. But with the same result. Not a chance. Too fat by half! Thus, the search for a pregnant sow, one close to farrowing, went unavailingly on its way. Till, annoyed by the stark, staring sterility of it all, the boss called out, 'Rouse 'em all and chase 'em around. Let's check each and every one of 'em. There must be at least one hiding itself away somewhere or other. Surely?

'Now, can you see one?' he asked, when the chase was done and the herd settled back into the

'None could be leaner,' I agreed.

freshly levelled straw. 'None whatsoever. I keep telling you, they are much too fat.'

Suddenly, his eyes lit up. 'How about that razor-backed, wry-necked, porcine plate-rack wheezing away in the corner? Don't tell me she's too fat!' 'None could be leaner,' I agreed. 'But it'll be a miracle if it farrows. It happens to be the bloody boar. He has his problems, too. I think he needs a rest!'

Spot Checks

THERE'S A tale to be told which plainly shows that the prospect of being spot checked is no more likely to deter a would-be miscreant than actually being caught out is likely to reform him.

Fairly late one evening during the very hot summer of 49, I was taking the girl, who was later to become my wife, for a spin around the country lanes in the pride o' my life: a battered, pre-war, crank-start Morris 8 van.

Here, for the sake of the younger reader, it needs to be stressed that in those days owning a vehicle of any description bordered on the miraculous; finding petrol to run it a miracle indeed! Petrol was sought after with zest and with hope, but rarely with success. A lucky few — mainly farmers and municipal dignitaries — received a quota. As for the rest, it was a matter of whoever fiddled best, travelled farthest!

Comparatively speaking I wasn't too badly off for petrol. I was working for the Herts War-Ag* who allowed me a gallon or two on an agricultural ticket — with the clear understanding that should I be caught using it for any purpose other than farming, I would be dealt with under the law (a heavy fine or imprisonment with hard labour). To help in its detection in case of misuse 'permit' petrol was coloured red.

So, on with my yarn. And there wouldn't be one to spin had I not stopped and tarried awhile to have a word with a workmate who I chanced to see working in a field alongside the road. I walked out to him.

'Guess who I have with me in my van tonight,' I said.

'No idea, George. But I've fair idea who it is standing beside it fiddling with the petrol filler cap.'

I looked back smartly at my van. 'Bloody hell! A plain clothes copper, checking on my petrol,' I spluttered, 'I'd better be going.'

'This yours?' snapped the man with the siphon.

'Yes,' I gulped.

'Mmmm . . . A commercial licence, I see. Aha . . Tanked up with red petrol too!'

'Yes,' I whimpered.

'Joy-riding!'

'No fear, mister. I'm on my way home from work. Late finishing tonight. Had a lot to do.'

'And the young lady?'

'Yes. She's a land-girl. I'm taking her back to her hostel. She's been working late, too.'

'Working late? Doing what?'

'Singling beet,' I lied.

'Does she always dress this way when she's singling beet? She looks as though she's off to a ball!' (I must admit, my passenger looked rather gorgeous in a print summer dress. Shiny, dark hair in ringlets cascading over her shoulders. Sun-tanned. As fresh as a mountain stream. A joy to behold!)

'Bloody hell! A plain clothes copper, checking on my petrol'

'She's fussy about her appearance, even at work,' I explained.

'I don't believe you,' said the cop. 'You're a liar, a scoundrel, and a criminal, too. You're in dead trouble, my lad. I must report you. Your name, please. And address? Good, Now your age.'

'Twenty nine,' I said.

'I want *your* age, not your father's.'

'Sorry, but I am twenty nine. Old enough, anyway, to have served in the Army right through the war.'

'Whereabouts?'

Trying not to sound boastful, I went through the list: from the Nile Delta in 1939 to the banks of the river Weser near Bremen on VE Day. His mood softened.

'Look. Do me a favour,' he commanded. 'Go home as fast as this shandy-barrow of yours can take you. Mention our meeting to no one, ever. Understand? Quick, off you go. You've had a close shave tonight. Very close indeed!'

I didn't need telling twice. Foot down hard, I was on my way. I jettisoned my passenger at the hostel gate and was back home indoors before the cop had time to tear a leaf out of his notebook.

'You look all shook up,' said my mum.

'I am. I've had a bit of a fright. But I'll soon recover; there's no doubt about that.'

And there wasn't. Such is the allure of a fair young maid when a young man's fancy lightly turns to thoughts of love. I was back outside the hostel again the next night, honking on my horn as loud as ever — even though my bride-to-be had offered neither to pay half the fine, nor serve her share of the prison sentence.

---

* Herts War Agricultural Executive Committee. A county body, with overwhelming authority on all matters concerning farming during and just after the war.

Murder in the Beanfield

'HOW COMES that when writing about your mates, George,' asks a reader, a stranger to our ways, 'you would have us all believe them to be genial fellows; kind and understanding; who would no more dream of drowning a kitten without first taking the chill off the water than baiting a mousetrap with anything but the tastiest cheese. Surely, in all your experience you must have met at least one farmworker who failed to measure up to your 'goodie-goodie' image?

Well, I must confess to meeting just one. A rash, brash, rumbustious ruffian, name of Reuben* (or Rubstone, as I came to call him — he was that abrasive). Now, he was an extraordinary fellow! Anyway, that's the way he struck me the moment I opened the door to his rat-a-tat tat, one Sunday morning just before harvest some twenty years ago.

'You the foreman?' he growled.

'Why . . . er . . . yes,' I replied.

'Reuben's the name. Rudd. The boss's sent me

---

* The names are fictitious, the people were real.

to introduce myself. I'm your new tractor bloke. Strictly arable. Never forget it. None of your bloody pigs for me! I don't like 'em and I don't like 'em as do. They tell me you're already in trouble over pig-men. So, let me tell you something, mate. You'll be in a bloody sight more trouble if you try swinging pigs on to me. Leave me the tractor work, and me and you'll get on all right. Bugger me about, and you'd be safer falling into a stone crusher. Understand? That's it, then. I'm off for a pint. See you tomorrow week.'

Numbed by the man and his manner, I stood transfixed in the doorway for quite some time after his departure, figuring out why Noah bothered to preserve two of Rubstone's kind from the Flood.

Built like a barrel, he bore the evidence of his forty years brawling etched upon his person. His most entertaining feature, I thought, was his protruding lower lip, from which constantly dangled a half lit cigarette dancing a fandango in time to every word he uttered, scattering ash over his expansive belly.

Although he was in his Sunday-best, it would be unfair of me to accuse him of being dressy. In actual fact, he was the first shirtless man I'd seen wearing a neatly knotted tie, raw, around his neck. An adornment which did little for his crumpled jacket, and even less for his beer-stained vest. He was fussy about his trousers, though, this was plain to see by the three attempts he had made at putting a crease in them. His boots had the sullen look of an

Army cook's. They'd obviously soaked up more sump-oil than an old brewer's drayman has supped old ale.

But enough of that. I'll pick up the story on the Monday he turned up ready to make a start. I set him to work, as far from the pigs as possible, with the heavy cultivator on 20 acres of fallow on the edge of the farm; and promised to give him a look in later on in the day. Thus it was that at three in the afternoon, on my way to see him. I happened upon his wife, Polly, taking him a can of tea and some tobacco he wanted.

'How much farther have I to go, Mr Scales?'

'Quite some way yet, Mrs Rudd. I'll take it if you like,' I said. She agreed with that, and followed on with the tobacco at a more leisurely pace.

Rubstone had stopped on the farmost side of the field when I reached him. He grabbed the can, then poured the tea down his throat as though he didn't like it and was swilling it down a drain. He wiped his mouth with the back of his hand, then bellowed to his wife.

'P-oll-oll-oll! Me bacca, P-oll-oll!' with a roar that made Tarzan's call sound like a bride's, 'I will.'

Polly fair flew over the clods to do his bidding. He snatched the tobacco, teased out the makings, rolled it into a cigarette, draped it on his bottom lip, lit up, then drove off at high speed to the exact spot where Polly had been standing when he called her over.

Poor Polly, I thought. And it was to be poor

George, too, long before harvest was out. I remember going into a field of laid barley to tell him, as delicately as I knew how, that he was leaving more grain in the field than was coming in on the trailers. He went stark raving mad. And, to my horror, rammed me into a ditch with his combine – flat out in top gear.

It was there that my guardian angel appeared unto me, as in a dream.

'Fear not,' said she. 'Though mighty dread hath seized thy troubled mind. Send Reuben forth to scare the crows; and leave dull care behind.'

She knew Rubstone's weakness, you see. He'd do anything for a spot of shooting. I set him up with a box of cartridges, and he sallied forth with a gun held together with snare-wire, as happy as someone who has won a foldaway mangle in a penny-raffle, not knowing that he was in for a mighty surprise.

Ricky Daniels was another in for a shock that afternoon. Ricky was our self-appointed game keeper by day, and a far-ranging poacher-supreme, by night. A lad who often boasted that God had made all creatures great and small for him to pot at.

The gunmen met at the wheatfield-edge. Rubstone was sauntering along dreaming of pigeon pie, when Ricky sprang from a thicket and, quite by accident knocked him sprawling. Rubstone was quick to react.

'Giddawf mee-land!' he bawled. 'Giddawf! D'y a hear!'

'Get off your what?' taunted Ricky, cockily. 'You haven't any, you landless peasant. Who are you, anyway?'

'I'll bloody soon show you who I am. Now giddawf!'

'Leave it out, grandad. Put your teeth in and give us a smile,' joked Ricky. That did it!

'BANG!' went Rubstone's gun. And the smoke arose from the smouldering earth at Ricky's feet.

'By Christ! You must be mad. You could have killed me,' quaked the young man.

'Giddawf! Or I'll blast every button off your weskit!'

Then 'BANG!' went the gun again. And Ricky felt the heat of the blast up his trouser leg as he dived for cover.

Rubstone's eyes sparkled with rare delight, that night, as he told the tale of the afternoon's 'Shoot-out'. He seemed almost chummy enough to discuss the finer points of combining.

He was up early the next day; but so was I — even earlier — and met him on his way — 'to get me a brace o' birds, while the dew comes off the barley,' as he put it. He'd barely finished speaking when there came a terrific 'BANG!' from a field of tics, close by.

'He's at it again!' cried Rubstone, in disbelief. Then cocked his gun and dashed into the beans, warning: 'Giddawf mee-land! Come out! Or I'll blow you out!' But there was no reply.

'All right, then. I can wait. You just try one shot more, and see.'

After a pause; 'BANG!' went the gun again and 'BANG!' went Rubstone's, swifter than an echo.

'You've killed poor Ricky,' I wailed.

'So what?' said the *murderer*, as he counted his cartridges and stormed off. I walked gingerly into the beans; and, not unexpectedly, found our carbide operated bird-scarer on its side, wheezing gas from its bellows and leaking water from its many tubes.

We soon restored it to normal, but not soon enough, however, for Rubstone to hear it explode again in anger. He was sacked within the week for roughing-up a spare-parts storeman, for supplying him with some RH shares he'd ordered that wouldn't fit the LH frog of his two-way plough.

I watched him depart, along with Polly, their chattels, and a dog called Butch. As they disappeared into the distance, I threw my hat, with glee, up into the sky. It landed high in a tree. Faded and torn, it hangs there yet. A constant reminder of the exception that proves the rule.

A *bird scarer*, resembling a mini-cannon, makes the noise without firing the ammunition. In early models the gas was produced by a mixture of carbide and water, but later models were fitted with propane gas. A relief valve could be set to cause detonations at set intervals. More sophisticated models were fitted with a time clock to ensure detonation would begin early in the morning at a time when the crops were most vulnerable to birds. *(Photograph courtesy of the Estate of Douglas Lawson)*

Ploughing Matches

PLOUGHING MATCHES really do get me down. Especially when I'm reminded how wildly popular they are with my mates who, I would have thought by now, should see them for the demeaning distraction they are and give them as wide a berth as they (my mates) tend to give our Wages Rally in Whitehall Place* every year.

It wouldn't be quite so bad if this unaccountably feverish desire to out-best each other at the commonest and most primitive job on earth affected only an isolated few. But nothing of the sort. It seems to be endemic. In all the time I've ploughed a forthright furrow, I've only met one other ploughman, a carefree son of the soil called Jim, who has shared my views on ploughing matches and the like.

But then Jim was a wise old boy. Wise enough, anyway, to have availed himself liberally of the joys of courting a publican's daughter for thirty odd years without allowing himself to get drunk enough to fancy marrying her.

Much wiser than Dick, another ploughman; a champion who shared the common view. He and Jim were forever arguing the toss about the worth of ploughing matches. I remember the morning in October 1949 when Dick came into work with the red card and what was left of the five shillings prize money he'd won at Saturday's ploughing match.

'That's the way to do it, Jim,' he said, flicking the card under Jim's nose. 'Like hell it is,' said Jim. 'I was watching you lot fiddling around out there on Saturday; and seeing as the judges were that fussy and you had so much time on your hands, I wonder they didn't give you a fork apiece and tell you to dig it.'

* Whitehall Place, home of the Ministry of Agriculture, is lobbied every year by farmworkers as national wage negotiations take place with the farmers.

A Moving Experience

 THE ONLY thing that worried me the day my wife and I brushed the confetti out of our hair and began married life together in our brand new home, was how the men in black were going to get the coffin down the narrow, twisting stairs when they eventually carried me out, feet first, at the end of an astoundingly long and contented life. But I needn't have bothered. I was out of the place, in mint condition, before I hardly had time to enjoy a couple of feeds of home-grown rhubarb.

Now, had that shock move been nothing worse than a hiccup on the way to a stable and, perhaps, distinguished career in agriculture, it would have been unsettling enough. But it marked the beginning of a wild bout of hiccupping that was to rattle my epiglottis for the next ten years or more. Even so, there was never to be another upheaval quite so uncalled for, as traumatic or (looking on the bright side) so intensely educational as the first.

I'll tell you a little about it. It might help some starry-eyed youngster presently thrilled at the thought of setting up home in a 'house that goes with the job' — as keen and green as I was exactly thirty six years ago today (15-10-85). Older readers, anyway, will appreciate just how green I was in those days when I confess to having had the house itself improved at my own expense before moving in. With permanency uppermost in my mind. I spent money I could ill-afford on fitting it out, too. All the time easing the pain of parting with hard-earned money, with the thought that it was a good investment in a promising future.

Every item purchased was carefully chosen, gently handled, expertly fitted and, finally, smugly admired.

Then, before our deep green curtains had a chance to fade, the boss called me into his office and told me that he wanted me out of his house!

'Nothing personal, Scales, I want you to understand,' he stumbled to explain. 'My problem is that I've had to sack MacKenzie, our head cowman, for bull-bashing. And as ill-luck would have it, he moved into one of the council's agricultural houses a short while ago and I can't get him out. To make matters worse, after he moved I let his cottage to a very dear friend of mine — a retired naval officer — and I can't get him out either. Not that I would want to in any case. He was torpedoed twice in the war. So you can see the fix I'm in; and why I must have your house for a cowman without delay. Now, now ... don't go upsetting yourself over it. It won't do any good. It's MacKenzie's fault really.

Curse the man! All that fuss about his being gored to death! I've never heard such a lame excuse. Never!'

I won't reduce you to tears (there were enough shed as it was) with the heart-rending details of our dismantling our lovely new home; I'll take up the story at the point where the removal van man was making his final inspection before moving off, and happened to spot me and Gina, our pet Alsation bitch, snuggling down in a cubbyhole I'd shaped out for us at the back of the van.

'That your bitch?' he asked.

'Why . . . yes.'

'She in season?'

'Yes, but . . . '

'Get her off. And no "buts" about it.'

Since there's little to be gained in arguing with

heartless authority when it has all your treasure in its keeping, I was forced to bike to our new place with Gina on tow behind.

Out in the wilds on a brisk day with a following wind the journey would have presented no problems at all. But on a sticky-hot June day heading into a stiffish breeze through a mainly residential area, alive with amorous hounds, it turned out to be an unforgettably exasperating affair indeed. So much so, it caused me to break the first golden rule of moving house: Be the last away from the old place and, even at the expense of drowning a litter of unwanted pups later on, be the first at the new. Delay spells chaos. And I was very, very late. The van was almost unloaded by the time we arrived.

On my way to lock Gina safely away from a couple of lusting labradors, I could see my ma-in-law through an open doorway hacking away at our supergrade, cork-backed, inlaid lino with a bread knife, seemingly piecing it up into a giant jigsaw puzzle. Then, just past the house (newly converted into workers' flats) I was hailed by a removal man stuck halfway up a whippy ladder with a gents wardrobe balanced precariously across his shoulders, hoping to get it in through an upstairs window.

'I can't hold on much longer, mate. Someone's got to help me. Either that, or I'll have to drop it,' he wailed.

'Don't falter. I'll be back in a minute.' I promised. But it was to be a long minute, because I was hindered first by the shepherd from number three, who wanted to know who said I could stand my high-rise hutches in front of his hollyhocks, and unbutton the doors to let my rabbits feast on his bedding plants; and then by the farm foreman. He was most upset.

'Those idiotic removal men have tipped your coal in my coalshed — on top of mine,' he griped.

'What! All half ton of it?' I asked.

'Half ton, be damned. There's barely that amount in there now, and I took delivery of five hundredweight only yesterday. We'd better split the lot — fifty-fifty.'

Feeling diddled, I shut Gina away, dashed into the house, over a blunted breadknife, up the stairs and braced myself at the opened window, ready to take a desperate heave at the wardrobe.

'A handy bloke to have at an awkward calving,' the removal man remarked, as he and the wardrobe toppled through the window and fell with a dull thud to the floor.

However, there was no time for me to wallow in such rare praise. Apart from rounding up the rabbits, there were a hundred and one things needing attention. Like the mother-in-law.

'Go and see what she wants,' ordered my wife, enshrouded in curtaining too long, too short or too narrow.

'I've got the lino down, George,' enthused her mum. 'All except the spare room. I can't do that, though. I've run out of tin tacks.'

'Tin tacks!?' I shrieked in alarm. 'Bloody tin tacks! Oh my God! My poor lino! You've crucified it!'

I could have wept. And very nearly did.

Early in July this year I reminded my wife of those turbulent times, as we sized up the very first offer — a wee bungalow — the local council has ever made to us in twenty years of our waiting for a house that doesn't go with the job.

'As small as it is, George,' she said, 'It could be worse. Anyway, there are no narrow, winding stairs. That should please you.'

It does. The saints be praised for that. On reflection, though, having taken a hard look at the shoe-box size bedroom, I think it best that I die standing up — on skids, facing the door.

Nicotiana Tabacum Avaunt!

I HAVE been toying with the idea —
once *Landworker* has finished with me
— of writing an article for both *The
Lancet* and *The Nursing Mirror* aimed at
helping those people from probationer nurse to
senior consultant, who ought to be setting a better
example by kicking the smoking habit but, although they would dearly love to, just can't.

On reflection, though, after reading Des Hales-
trap's letter in the November issue of our new-
paper, and while I'm still smarting from the rebuke
in the supplement about us not minding our own
business enough, I think it better that I leave the
medical profession to its own devices, let charity
begin at home and, instead, set about helping any
Landworker reader who happens to be baffled by the
same smouldering problem.

Probably, that reader is you.

If that's the case, read on. You may bless the
day.

To begin with, you may be interested to learn
that the reason why your problem smoulders on, is

that in the past you've set out to stop smoking for ever. I reckon you've been asking far too much of yourself. From now on, what you want to do is to see what length of time you can put between stubbing out your last cigarette and lighting up another. Whether that smokeless interlude lasts only an hour or stretches into years depends very much upon your sticking to these two basic essentials: Never be over-ambitious; nor set at naught your own proven ability.

And the first thing to prove is that you can forego that first, desperate smoke of the day, and still survive. Now, before moving on to what would be your second smoke of the day, there are one or two tips which, from personal experience, I know will prove most helpful.

Keep well stocked up with cigarettes and matches. Remember — Absence, in the case of cigarettes, really does make the heart grow fonder!

Another thing — Beware of those who would scoff at your intentions. Keep them in the dark. Now is the time for quiet resolve. Don't be like the show-off I once knew who, with measured tread made his way to the local Bridge-of-sighs then, with heroic gesture, hurled his cigarettes, his pipe, his tobacco pouch, lighter and matches, one after the other, over the parapet into the swirling waters below, loudly proclaiming: 'Not withstanding my former enslavement to Demon Nicotine, henceforth, not even my compost heap will I defile with that obnoxious weed — *Nicotiana Tabacum!'*

Old Show-off was to be seen downstream in the early morning light the next day, furtively dredging the shallows, anxiously trying to salvage the more durable items he had disposed of at the cleansing ceremony the day before.

Fascination in a challenge is a thing of substance, and will easily outlast the wildest demonstration.

Returning now to that 'second' smoke. Usually, the one that goes down so well straight after breakfast. To manage without that can be almost as painful as foregoing the first. But not so much so that it can't be eased by your new-found assurance firmly based on the fact that you've already overcome the most daunting part of the exercise. Just say to yourself: If I can manage to master the urge to smoke for an hour before breakfast, there's no sensible reason why I can't hold out for an hour after.

Thus you begin to build on success. Taking the positive view. Knowing that what is within your grasp is not beyond your reach.

Next, without being over-ambitious, you may safely assume that your first two smokeless hours can be stretched to four. This should lead to your going the best part of the morning without a smoke. With the morning behind you, you can begin to look forward to testing your resolve well on into late afternoon. So far, so good. The evening may be tricky though. But don't let your resolve founder on the idle moment. That would be a silly waste of an exceedingly good day's work.

Stand firm. Then, if at bedtime, it pleases you to say the day went well and that you're determined tomorrow will go equally well, you have successfully opened the way to your counting the time between your last smoke and the next, not by the hour (as at first) but by the day, the week, the month and the year.

I stubbed out my last cigarette late on Christmas night in 1944, and to date, have managed to resist the temptation to light another. Boxing day was agony, though, but well worth the pain.

If a weak-willed chain-smoker like me can hold out for 41 years, there's no reason why you can't. Especially these days when there's evidence enough to prove that smoking can have a devastating effect upon your health. It really is a killer.

So go to it. And good luck. Oh, by the way, should you get the chance, do slip a spare copy of this month's *Landworker* in with the usual rubbishy stuff that litters the table in your doctor's waiting room. It might help another about to succumb to the 'weed.'

It might even help the doctor himself.

We had a Dream

WHENEVER FOLK around me start talking about the Welfare State as though it is a wanton extravagance, my thoughts wing back to the Desert War. To my being pinned down by intense enemy artillery and mortar fire (plus a few strays of our own!) out in the open, a hundred yards or so into nomans land, in the opening phase of that ill-starred campaign — code name: *Crusader*. We — that is a company of attacking infantry, and a few odd-bods such as myself whom they'd picked up for various reasons on the way — hit the deck, without choosing our spot, at seven in the morning. We were still there at four in the afternoon.

In that, the most pulverising nine hours I'm ever likely to experience; besides assessing and reassessing over and over again the likelihood of my surviving, and not ending up as a name on our village war memorial, or another claimant on the Poppy Day Appeal Fund, I remember staring in stupified fascination at the barrage itself. An unusual sight which, despite its awful threat, at times had something about it akin to beauty.

I thought so, anyway, as salvo after salvo came screaming in, crashing down and erupting; sending dust and debris pluming up into the steel-blue winter sky; holding it there just long enough to catch the light and display its more pleasing aspects before it filtered down through the smoke back to earth; flushing away the dun, the russet and apricot shades; leaving instead a surly, drab-black curtain hanging above the desert, ready for the next salvo to shock it into a confusion of animated shapes and shades all over again.

Although I was the last man that day who was likely to stand up and applaud the performance, I couldn't help marvelling at the awesome spectacle.

Turning to a mate lying nearby, a fellow we called Ginger, who, at that moment, was not alone in wishing that he'd been born an armadillo and not a child of an Empire on which the sun never sets; I shouted:

'What a show! And it's all for us, too! It must be costing the earth! Just think what could be done when the war is won if we started spending money on the same scale on things that really matter!'

'That day can't come too soon for me, chum,' he yelled back. 'There must be a better way of spending it than like this. Yet we never seem . . . '

Poor old Ginger. He didn't live to see the start we made on breathing life into that lofty ideal we called the Welfare State. But he would have approved; there is no doubt. Just as today he would weep to see the way we have failed to cherish it, and how we seem content to hand it over to jugglers and clowns and people wanting to help fund it for a bit of a giggle.

Vacant Situations

 IN MY eyes, job hunting will forever remain a 'pig in a poke' affair. Full of disappointments and surprises. Especially surprises.

Surprises came thick and fast in my formative years on English farms. I landed my first job in the most astonishing of circumstances. I turned up for the interview only to find my employer-to-be head and shoulders down in a man-hole tinkering with a stopcock. He didn't think it worth his while to raise his head above ground level to speak to me; so I was unable to tell whether the man who 'would employ me' was clean-shaven or had a beard trailing his knees.

'Start on Monday. Seven sharp,' came his echoed instructions from the chamber below.

Keen to get going, I was at his place well before seven on the day. So early, in fact, that there was only one other person — a far from distinguished looking individual I took to be the swillman — to be seen anywhere around. 'What time does that scraggy-necked old ostrich come out?' I asked him.

'Time enough to catch anyone who's late! I sack those who are!' he rapped.

Beware the call from afar, as well. The best jobs rarely need to be advertised, not even locally. They usually get snapped up by those living down-wind with a well developed sense of smell.

Tread lightly, too, where box numbers are concerned. Vacancies flitting around in a box number disguise can sometimes turn out to be too close for comfort. I knew an occasion where a fool rushed in and unwittingly applied for his own job. It didn't help matters, either, when he asked for travelling expenses to go and take a look at it!

Dinner at Gran's

NOT SO long ago, listeners to a radio phone-in were asked what they thought was meant by the term Victorian values. Although the response was widespread, I thought the answers that were given fell short of the true meaning. As viewed from below, anyway.

Since this piece sees the end of my extended stay with our journal, I'll take my leave with a personal, family story. A story I've been awaiting an opportune moment to tell. It's about a Sunday dinner, which taught me, at the age of six, all I want to know about Victorian values.

Gran, that's my dad's mum, was left a widow with a family of ten the year that Queen Victoria died. Now, in a story book, one of high moral tone typical of the time, the author would have had gran struggling bravely on against almost insurmountable odds, working her fingers to the bone caring for her children; an angel without wings; making their little home a haven in a hostile world. In reality, though, things didn't turn out that way at all.

Like many another poor bewildered soul in those inglorious days of devout hypocrisy, when greed and piety wreaked their own particular distortions on working-class folk, gran sought solace in drink, old ale. And she didn't do things by half, either. People outside the family called her a sot. I prefer to call her a victim of circumstances. Her fifth son, my father, couldn't bring himself to talk about his mother seriously in any respect.

'It was unusual to see her outside an inn,' he'd quip, forcing a pun, just leaving it at that.

'Gran called in today. She's asked us over to dinner,' my mum said to my dad one evening as he came in from work. 'I suppose we ought to go. Oughtn't we?' she added.

'Suit yourself. I'm game.'

'Game? What do you mean by that?'

'You'll see,' said dad.

Thus it came about one Sunday morning in the autumn of 1926, our little family group was to be seen heading toward the sound of church bells in the neighbouring village, on our way to gran's.

The bells had long since ceased to ring by the time we arrived.

Dad knocked on the door. There was no reply. He knocked again. Still nothing.

'I wonder where she is?' whispered mum, half expecting to find Gran slaving over a hot stove.

'Not in church. That's for sure,' said dad, as he pushed open the door and called out.

'Anyone in? You there, ma?'

Cowman and gardener's daughter wed, Potters Bar, 1926. *(Gran is on the far right)*

All remained quiet inside. So, after ushering us into the house, he set off in search of his mum.

Other than a piece of sacking on the stone floor by the back door, and some tattered lace curtaining strung across the window, the room was bare. A fly-flecked mirror advertising Dewar's whisky rested on a ledge above a cheerless hearth, on each side of which stood an upturned beer crate. The whole place reeked of stale beer and doused firewood.

It wasn't long before dad returned. He'd managed to rustle up every non-churchgoer in the village, except his own mother. But none of them appeared to be bothered about her, as they crowded in through the door to size us up before spilling out again, leaving one of their number behind to see to the fire.

No sooner had they gone, they reappeared. In file, this time. Led by two strong lads carrying a polished-top table; then four people with a chair apiece; another with a special chair for my eldest sister, a toddler at the time; someone handed my brother and me a cushion each for our chairs to raise us chin-above-plate level; a woman came in next, she had a tablecloth and was trying her best to get a little girl to come forward with cutlery all wrapped in a yellow duster; a buxom lass brought in the condiments and a jug of water; her friend, five tumblers and a vase of chrysanths; then the two lads paid another call, this time with a wind-up gramophone and an assortment of records, as well as a clock, with the instructions that it kept good time if laid on its back.

After we had arranged ourselves around the table, the 'caterers' appeared upon the scene, and hastily began serving up a piping hot, delicious looking Sunday roast that had been rushed in from a house halfway up the alley.

With scant regard for culture, dad cut short Dame Nellie Melba's rendering of the inappropriate 'Home Sweet Home' on a Winner record, replaced it with a rousing march on a Decca, slung some salt over his dinner like he was gritting an icy road, rubbed his hands together then, in the way of grace, loudly exclaimed:

'Get stuck in, lads, Christmas is early this year!'

We didn't need telling twice; we soon made short work of the roast; as indeed we did the sweet that followed. We managed, however, to sip the tea that was brought in to round off the meal at a more leisurely pace, helped, no doubt, by a sleepy waltz tune on the gramophone called 'Drifting and Dreaming' I think.

But once our cups were empty, things began to move. In the other direction this time. Far quicker than they arrived. Till only the clock and the gramophone remained.

'Have a heart,' pleaded dad, as they moved towards the melody maker. 'Take the bloody clock if you like. It's lost five minutes already, but let's have a bit of music, for christsake!'

Gran came in at three. You could see she had been singing, her face was cherry red. She was wearing a sloppy cardigan sporting pockets like pack-saddles, each weighted down almost to the ground with a quart bottle of ale. Once she had teased the bottles from her pockets and set them down within easy reach on the floor, she lowered herself down upon a beer crate, sighed a long drawn out sigh, and dozed off.

She awoke with a start. Then, remembering the invitation, she asked us if we had been attended to all right. Dad nodded. 'Then yurrel be shtayin' for tea, woan you,' she slurred, and informed us that it had all been paid for. A deciding factor that, where gran was concerned; for she quite believed it fully committed us to stay.

'Sorry, gran. But we really must be on our way,' mum replied, rather huffily. Mum was 'Band of Hope' you see, and a sworn enemy of Demon Drink.

She really gave poor old dad the rough side of her tongue on the way home.

'Humiliating! That's what it was,' she scolded. 'Making beggars of us!'

'Beggars be damned,' dad countered, not showing the slightest remorse. 'I've begged from some of those kind neighbours when I was a lad, and I know 'em! They wouldn't see you starve. Oh no! They'd look the other way. It's surprising how the chinkle of a coin can soften hearts as hard as theirs.'

Thirty years on, just before he died, I asked him if he remembered that extraordinary meal.

'Like it was yesterday,' he said. And, not for the first time, went on to tell me about his boyhood days. A boyhood of begging, borrowing and stealing to stay alive. How, in wintertime, he and his brothers would sleep huddled together under old corn sacks in a cupboard for warmth. How they'd get up in the morning, shake themselves 'like a dog', take a swig at the village pump, then chase off around the houses begging for scraps.

'How did you go on about cleaning your teeth, dad?' I asked.

'Bless my soul, boy, we never had anything in our mouths long enough to dirty 'em,' he replied. 'Like pearls they were!'

Apparently, oral hygiene was another of those things the Victorians valued!

End

SO, THAT'S it. I really must be going. Maybe, we'll meet again. Some other time; some other place. Take good care of yourselves; and thank you. Your forbearance has been magnificent.

Wasted Prayers

When kneeling at night by your bedside,
Beseeching The Lord for more pay,
Remember he deals only with rich men by night
Then drops off to sleep in the day.

(Photograph courtesy of the Estate of Douglas Lawson)